Food for Thought

Food for Thought

BRINGING ESTATE PLANNING TO LIFE

JEAN BLACKLOCK · JUDY MIYASHIRO · SUSAN MURPHY

JOHN WILEY & SONS CANADA, LTD.

Toronto • New York • Chichester • Weinheim • Brisbane • Singapore

John Wiley & Sons Canada, Ltd.
22 Worcester Road
Etobicoke, Ontario M9W 1L1
Visit our Web site at: www.wiley.com/canada

National Library of Canada Cataloguing in Publication Data
Blacklock, Jean, 1961–
    Food for thought : bringing estate planning to life

ISBN 0-471-64644-X

1. Estate planning—Canada—Popular works. I. Miyashiro, Judy. 1965– II. Murphy, Susan, 1947– III. Title.

KE5974.Z82B58 2001   346.7105'2   C2001-9901812-6

Production Credits
Cover Design and Text: Interrobang Graphic Design Inc.
Printing and Binding: Tri-Graphic Printing Limited

Printed and bound in Canada
10 9 8 7 6 5 4 3 2 1

Contents

Preface

WE LIVE IN THE EASIEST OF TIMES. With our automatic garage-door openers and our microwave approach to fine dining, "hard" is a four-letter word, in more ways than one. But in our hearts we know that not everything can, or should, be easy. Why, for example, should we expect estate planning to be easy, simple, or cheap? As we blend our families, dancing with new partners while still raising children from previous relationships, our lives become complicated. So, too, shall our deaths unless we take the time and trouble to consider our financial and legal affairs in advance.

Contrary to common wisdom, even the most "apple-pie" family can present important estate planning choices and challenges. This is said not to scare you, but to encourage you to seek help in the appropriate places. Taking care of your own estate planning is a little like getting under the hood of your own car—you're likely fine when it comes to topping up fluid levels but do you really want to get into fixing the brakes? While most of us have a basic understanding of the internal combustion engine, we still prefer to get our cars fixed by a trained mechanic—someone who is intimately acquainted with our particular make and model, someone who is skilled at diagnosing and preventing other potential problems.

Instinctively, we know making a mistake can be very costly. But since not one of us plans to die tomorrow, what's wrong with putting off dealing with the problem? The trouble is, a little bit of procrastination can go a very long way. It's a sad reality that people *do* die unexpectedly, children *are* left without named guardians, parents *do* become incapacitated. When we're caught up in the daily business of living our lives, most of us try to avoid contemplating these possibilities. But avoidance, far from freeing us from these concerns, leaves us instead with a nagging feeling of unease. When something happens—say, a fellow worker collapses with a heart attack—we resolve to get our own affairs in order, but the moment passes and we fall back into inactivity.

While estate planning is not necessarily easy, simple, or cheap, neither is it necessarily difficult, complicated, or expensive. Once you've completed the process, those 3 a.m. moments of panic can be replaced by the calm knowledge that your affairs are in order, your loved ones will be protected, your wishes will be carried out. Put this way, most people can see the benefits—the trouble lies in how to get started, how to overcome that completely understandable inertia and take the first steps. It is my hope that this book will be the catalyst you need.

Food for Thought is not a guide to planning your estate in three "easy" lessons. It acknowledges that a trained professional—one who is sensitive to your own particular circumstances—will likely always be your best source of advice. But in order for you to maximize the time you spend with a professional, or for you even to see the wisdom of contacting her or him in the first place, you need to have an appreciation of the issues. *Food for Thought* takes you by the hand and allows you to listen in on a group of people coming to terms with the kind of estate planning questions we all face.

The bimonthly meetings of the Elderberry Gate Dinner Club are an opportunity for fellow residents to share food and practical concerns—all leavened with a healthy dose of laughter. And, while the characters may be fictional, the issues are only too real.

First, allow me to introduce you to the residents of Elderberry Gate, then kick off your shoes and spend some time at the party—you'll probably be glad that you did!

Jean Blacklock
Calgary, Alberta

Members

OF THE ELDERBERRY GATE DINNER CLUB

- **Gerald** and **Vanessa Porter**   2 Elderberry Gate

Gerald is a cardiologist and Vanessa is a volunteer in a number of community initiatives. The Porters are in their 60s and each has adult children from previous marriages.

- **Fiona McCarthy**   4 Elderberry Gate

Fiona has recently retired from her position as an executive with an oil company. At the age of 57, Fiona has never married. As an only child, Fiona is responsible for the care of her widowed father, Ronald McCarthy.

- **Todd Reimer** and **Nori Okawa**   6 Elderberry Gate

Todd and Nori are "common-law" partners who do not have children, either as a couple, or from previous relationships. Todd, aged 38, is divorced, but Nori, 36, has never married. They are in business together, owning and operating Nori's Home and Botanical, a gift boutique and florist.

- **Doug** and **Sheila Enright**   8 Elderberry Gate

The Enrights are in their mid-40s. Doug is in middle management of a large corporation and Sheila is a speech pathologist. They have been married 20 years and have a son, Jason, who is a freshman at the University of British Columbia.

ACKNOWLEDGEMENTS

THE WRITING OF A BOOK SUCH AS THIS HAS MUCH IN COMMON WITH THE PROCESS OF ESTATE PLANNING. Both activities involve a good deal of thought, discussion, and soul searching and, as might well be expected, the occasional false step along the way. Whether writing a will or writing a book, we have discovered it is wise to seek help from persons who are experts in their field. We hope that reaching your goal will be a richly rewarding experience. Certainly, as authors, collaborators, and friends, we have found this to be the case.

Along the way, we have had assistance and support from many quarters. In particular, we would like to thank the following: Robyn Hawkins of BMO Harris Private Banking, Toronto for assistance with the legal research; Judi Leong, Marlene Rae, and Gail Boldt of Penta Graphix Ltd. of Calgary for their professional assistance; Kim Bernbaum for her creative input; and Ron Nowell of the Calgary Herald for his continued interest. Our largest debt of gratitude is to BMO Harris Private Banking for its generous support of our project.

On a more personal note, we would also like to acknowledge the support and love of our spouses, Don Higa, Eldon Rawleigh, and Neil Murphy and our families and friends. We couldn't have done it without you!

Jean Blacklock
Judy Miyashiro
Susan Murphy
Calgary, Alberta

September

A *Fall* FEAST

"SEPTEMBER. SEASON OF MISTS AND MELLOW FRUITFULNESS," THOUGHT VANESSA AS SHE PLACED A POT OF BRONZE CHRYSANTHEMUMS IN THE STONE URN BY THE FRONT DOOR OF HER CONDOMINIUM. "Close bosom friend of the maturing sun…" Transported back to her Grade 9 classroom at Bishop Strachan School for Girls, she struggled to come up with a few more lines from Keats's ode. "To set budding more and still more, later flowers for the bees until they think warm days will never cease for…for…they obviously don't live in Calgary where we're lucky we haven't had snow by now!"

Smiling, Vanessa closed the door. No point, she thought, in anticipating the cold days ahead. Better to celebrate the fact that the Farmers' Market was still in full swing and that she had a dinner party to plan. Settling herself in a chair, she sipped from a cup of Earl Grey tea and luxuriated in the clear yellow sunlight flooding her kitchen. Full of anticipation, she adjusted her reading glasses and reached for the topmost volume of a teetering pile of cookbooks.

The Porters were the most senior residents of Elderberry Gate and while Vanessa—a youthful 60 year old—would shudder at the thought of herself as a matriarchal figure, she nonetheless had assumed somewhat of a leadership role in the residents' activities. Years of establishing and leading volunteer boards had given her a kind of roll-up-your-sleeves practicality coupled with the ability to draw out the best from everyone with whom she dealt. She had that enviable quality of making things happen, which was no doubt the reason she was hosting the first meeting of the new season's Elderberry Gate Dinner Club.

An hour and three cups of tea later, Vanessa had inserted more than a dozen hot-pink sticky-notes in the pages of her cookbooks and had whittled down her choice of a main course to a curried pork tenderloin.

"Hi, Helen! It's Vanessa—may I speak to Gerald, please? Oh, well, whenever he's got a moment. I plan to be home for the rest of the morning."

As the wife of a cardiologist, Vanessa was used to standing in line to grab a few moments of her husband's time. She really did not like to break into his surgery hours, but she couldn't remember having asked Gerald to enter the date of the dinner club meeting in his Day-Timer. Now she had to keep her fingers crossed that he hadn't made plans to fly off to some conference or symposium. Even if he hadn't made any conflicting plans, Vanessa knew he would like some time to ponder the wine selection. Unlike some of their younger friends, Gerald left all the food preparation to his wife but he did pride himself on being something of an oenophile. Just as Vanessa liked to mull over recipes, so Gerald liked to play with the possibilities of the perfect wine accompaniment.

"Oh hi, Gerald! I just wanted to remind you about the dinner club meeting a week next Saturday. No, of course I didn't think you'd forgotten … just wanted to let you know I've decided on pork—curried tenderloin, actually. Yes, I realize curry's a bit of a challenge—we could always go with beer if you can't think of anything better. No? Well, I'll leave it in your capable hands. And speaking of capable hands, I've asked Miriam Perlman to drop in on her way home from work for a drink. I wanted to ask her professional opinion about an article I read on estate planning. Are you still playing squash after work? Well, don't take too long in the sauna and you'll be able to say hello. I hope you won't be too ravenous after your game— it's just leftovers tonight, I'm afraid, but I do have some lovely ripe pears. We'll have them with a bit of Stilton for dessert!"

ↂ

Some people are naturally organized; Vanessa Porter did not count herself among them. As a child she had revelled in summers at the lake where no one had told her to keep her room tidy or even to remove from under her bed the cluster of murky, smelly jars containing valuable specimens of aquatic life. As a student at university, she had been the one forever searching for the misplaced quotation or reading list, the one who would wail, "I know it's here somewhere!" In her first job in public relations, she had come close to getting fired for accidentally shredding a crucial document, and that incident had proved to be a turning point. As a matter of professional pride, she had willed herself into being an organized person. It was a commitment that had continued to serve her well and by this point in her life, her methodical ways had become almost, but not quite, ingrained. Bookshelves on her kitchen wall held numerous three-ring binders, all neatly labelled. One volume entitled "Retirement/Estate Planning" was filled almost to overflowing with articles clipped from the financial pages of newspapers and magazines. In preparation for Miriam's visit, Vanessa re-read an article that had recently piqued her interest and placed it on the living room's polished walnut coffee table.

⚬⚭⚬

"Hi Miriam! Thanks for dropping by," said Vanessa as she motioned her old friend into a comfortable chair in the living room. "What would you like—red wine, white wine, sherry…?" "A nice dry sherry would be just wonderful—in fact, anything would be wonderful after the day I've had. It's great to relax for a moment. I hope you don't have anything too taxing to ask me!" Vanessa passed the clipped newspaper column to Miriam. "Take a quick look at this—if you haven't already seen it—and I'll rustle up some nibblies. I don't know about you but I'm famished!"

While Vanessa busied herself in the kitchen, Miriam quickly skimmed the newspaper article. Like Vanessa, she made a point of reading newspaper columns on estate planning if for no other reason than self-protection. Miriam's clients often came into her office clutching copies of the latest column to hit the stands, saying, "This business in the paper—does it apply to me?"

Returning to the living room with a dish of pistachios, Vanessa said, "I remember when Gerald and I got married you were kind enough to remind us that we needed to redo our wills. That was almost two years ago and I'm embarrassed to say that we haven't exactly jumped at your advice."

"You're not alone, let me assure you," said Miriam with a laugh. "Most of my clients seem to put writing a will right up there with getting a root canal or being audited by the tax department!" "Seeing that newspaper column reminded me that we should really make an effort to get on top of the situation. In fact, I plan to call your office first thing tomorrow morning to set up an appointment for the two of us to come in. But in the meantime, I wanted to ask you about the spousal trust business that's mentioned in the article. I think Gerald once said something about establishing one but in this column, the writer seems to have some reservations. I'm not sure I even understand what a spousal trust is. If Gerald set one up, would it be to protect his children or me? Or could it do both at once?"

"How much time do you have?" asked Miriam, smiling, as she set her sherry aside and sat forward in her chair. "It's quite complicated and I think we should reserve all of the ins and outs for when you and Gerald come to see me in my office. However, I suspect that when you invited me to drop by tonight you weren't looking for a full treatise on the subject, but rather a woman-to-woman assurance that a spousal trust wouldn't be against your better interests. And, what's more, you were savvy enough to want to ask the question without Gerald being around."

"Am I that transparent? Of course, I trust Gerald implicitly to be fair, it's just that…"

"You've already had first-hand experience of being widowed," Miriam said, finishing her friend's thoughts, "and it's quite understandable that you have some concerns. When Charles died, there were a whole lot of problems that could have been avoided with a little bit of forethought."

Vanessa smiled ruefully. "You can say that again. I don't know what I would have done without the help of friends like you. Or without the odd glass of sherry, come to think of it! Can I refresh your glass?"

"No thanks, I'm fine and I should be on my way before too long. Let me explain that a spousal trust is often entered into when the person signing a will is in a second marriage. Typically, it's a way of ensuring that the surviving spouse has ample assets to benefit from during his or her lifetime while at the same time directing that the remaining assets pass to the children from the first marriage upon the spouse's death."

"If Gerald dies first, shouldn't he just trust me to do the right thing? Surely, he wouldn't think that I would pass on *his* money to my kids and leave his own children out in the cold?"

"Knowing you as well as I do, I would say that Gerald doesn't have a thing to worry about, but that's not really the point. No one can predict the future, and circumstances can, and do, change. At one time, no one believed the *Titanic* would ever sink but the rest, as they say, is history."

"You said something about the surviving spouse having enough money during his *or* her lifetime. I suppose that means I could set up a spousal trust, too, so that if I die first, I could be sure that *my* assets would eventually pass to Sarah and Caroline rather than to Gerald's children."

"Yes, that's right. Of course, at one time, it was usually the husband who had sole control of a couple's finances and a spousal trust in some ways allowed him to continue controlling his estate after death. Nowadays, it's much more common for each marriage partner to take equal responsibility for financial decisions and, of course, it is more likely that a woman will have assets in her own name than it ever was in the past."

"It sounds like spousal trusts are quite old-fashioned. Why would anyone bother with them anymore?"

"The situation you're in with Gerald is a classic example—each of you has children from a previous marriage and assets in your own names."

"I guess I can see what you're getting at. It seems like a spousal trust might be a good idea because in a complicated arrangement like a second marriage, it sets everything out in writing and avoids a lot of problems down the road. I can't bear the thought of ever getting into a dispute with John or Lucy. They're just like my own kids to me."

"Before you get too gung-ho on the idea, let me point out that a spousal trust is not without its downside. In fact, the points made in this column are good ones. Often, people have the idea that trusts somehow look after themselves, but that's not true at all. Their on-going care and maintenance typically require one or more trustees, the annual filing of trust tax returns, the advice and services of both an accountant and a lawyer, to say nothing of good communication among all parties concerned. Obviously, it's not something to rush into without considering all the consequences. But that's all the advice you're going to get from me tonight. I'll look forward to hearing from you tomorrow. Tell Gerald he'll have to free himself up for an afternoon and check his beeper at the door! Thanks for the drink and give my love to Sarah and Caroline when you see them."

∽⊙⊙∼

Saturday morning—the day of the Elderberry Gate Dinner Club meeting—Vanessa woke with a sense of pleasant well-being. She could hear Gerald puttering in the kitchen and thought if she waited long enough she might be rewarded with a cappuccino and the review section of the weekend paper. Looking through the window at the golden leaves of the poplar trembling in the breeze, she reflected on all that she had done in the previous week. First, her property committee had helped finish painting the community hall and then she had been lucky enough to find a major sponsor for the Juvenile Diabetes fundraiser. Then there had been the visit to Miriam Perlman, who, as usual, had been tremendously helpful and had laid out all they needed to know regarding spousal trusts. Giving themselves some time to mull over their options, there was still a good chance that both their wills would be signed and sealed before their second wedding anniversary in November. What a relief to have dispensed with that nagging feeling of unfinished business! Finally, there was the satisfaction that came from having organized the menu for the dinner party in good time and having delivered all the recipes to the participants with a week to spare. This issue had been up for debate during the formation of the club—should the host provide the others with recipes to follow or should each couple bring something they had decided upon? Vanessa had held out for the host providing recipes to the others and, for the most part, her view had prevailed. Not only did it stretch people to try something they might normally never make but it also resulted in a better-balanced menu.

"Oh, Gerald—aren't you a sweetheart? You must have known I was thinking if you really loved me you would bring me a cappo."

"You mean you thought if you lay there long enough the chances were I'd break down and do battle with that bloody machine," said Gerald, plumping up the pillows behind Vanessa's head and handing her the newspaper.

"There you go again, pretending you're a techno-peasant." She sipped from the cup. "Mmm … this coffee is great and you've managed to get tons of foam."

"You've got most of it on your upper lip, you silly thing. Better let me kiss it off… there, that's better. And just for the record, why were you grinning like a Cheshire cat when I brought the coffee in? Do you get some kind of sadistic pleasure thinking of me as a rookie barista?"

"No, I was actually thinking of that hilarious pot luck we went to at your sister's when just about everyone brought a dish made with spinach. Don't you remember? We brought Oysters Rockefeller, Peter and Sally did a spinach salad, George had picked up some spanokopita, and someone else had brought a spinach lasagna. It was a wonder we didn't all clank as we left—we must have had so much iron in our systems!"

"I'd forgotten about that," said Gerald. "Thank God we've got the Queen of Organization looking after everything tonight. Speaking of tonight—is there anything you want me to pick up besides a couple of baguettes?"

"Can't think of anything. Oh, wait a minute. I do need some fresh ginger, if you wouldn't mind stopping by the supermarket. Not the powdered stuff in jars but the light brown knobby stuff you find in the produce department. Think you can handle that?"

⌒⌒⌒

With Gerald dispatched on his errands, Vanessa had a quick shower, pulled on some jeans and a sweatshirt, and did a brief tour of inspection of the condominium. It never ceased to amaze her how clean and tidy a place could stay when there were no children (of any age) in residence. There were many times when Vanessa looked back fondly to when her daughters, Sarah and Caroline, were young. What she did not recall with the same degree of pleasure were the peanut butter sandwiches that had been surreptitiously fed into the slot of the VCR or the collection of crayons, marbles, and Play-Doh pellets that were a constant presence in the depths of the sofa cushions. Satisfied that everything was shipshape and that all the ingredients for her part of the dinner were safely stowed in the fridge (with the exception, of course, of the fresh ginger), Vanessa turned to the part of the dinner preparations that she loved the best—making the table beautiful.

But before she turned to her collection of heirloom linens—many passed on to her from her mother, and her mother before her—Vanessa went outside and tapped on the door of her next-door neighbour, Fiona McCarthy. Fiona was a recently retired oil company executive whose busy career had kept her from ever learning how to entertain at home.

She used to joke that the only thing she was good at making was reservations but now that she had a lot more time on her hands, Fiona was determined to develop some domestic talents.

"Hi, Fiona. What are you up to?"

"Hey, Vanessa—good timing. I've been looking at the salad recipe you gave me and wondering how the heck I get the zest out of a lemon."

"That wasn't very smart of me. I should have realized you likely wouldn't own a lemon zester. I guess there isn't too much call for that particular piece of equipment in the oilpatch! I was actually coming over to ask whether you'd like to give me a hand setting the table. Why don't you bring your lemon along and we can kill two birds with one stone?"

Back inside Vanessa and Gerald's condo, Fiona was very impressed by Vanessa's collection of table linens, which she kept in a large pine chest.

"Gee—look at that! All pressed and starched and ready to go. How come everything's wrapped in tissue?"

"It's supposed to help minimize the creases. I remember when my grandmother lived in her big house in Toronto, she had a butler's pantry with large wooden rollers to store her tablecloths on so they never had to be folded. Of course, those were the days before condo living!"

In a few moments, Vanessa's large oval mahogany table was draped, almost to the floor, with a creamy, iridescent cloth.

"Wow, it's beautiful!" said Fiona.

"Ah, yes—but we've only begun. Let's do the flowers next. I picked up some lovely gerbera daisies from Nori's flower shop."

Twenty minutes later, the table looked like an ode to autumn. Orange and yellow gerberas in a row of single blossom vases ran down the centre of the table. Under Vanessa's guidance, Fiona had strewn baby pumpkins, tiny gourds, and miniature cobs of dried Indian corn in the spaces in between. As a finishing touch, the women had stripped the kernels from one of the corncobs and scattered them on the tablecloth.

"It looks like something out of a magazine," said Vanessa. "Good job, Fiona!"

"Yeah, pretty soon I'll have Martha Stewart shaking in her boots! That is, once I've learned how to zest a lemon."

⋘◦⦿◦⋙

Promptly at 7 p.m. on Saturday, the other residents of Elderberry Gate stood at the entrance to the Porters' variously clutching an assortment of plastic bowls, baskets of crackers, and intriguing foil-wrapped packages. Partly, their high spirits were derived from the fact that they hadn't been together for three months and there was a lot of catching up to be done. And partly, no matter how often they met, there was always the anticipation of tasting new foods, drinking new wines, and learning new things about each other.

"Come in, come in," said Vanessa. "It's lovely to see you all. Gerald, Sheila looks like she's about to drop dessert—can you give her a hand, please?"

"Yes, *do* let me take that from you, Sheila. I'm sure you don't want to see a grown man cry!" Having safely stowed Doug and Sheila Enright's dessert in the refrigerator, Gerald efficiently filled everyone's drink orders. In the meantime, Vanessa suggested that Todd and Nori might wish to serve their appetizer during the discussion of condo business (which, as they had to remind themselves, *was* the official reason for their get-together).

Time passed quickly with the sharing of summer experiences. Fortunately, there was very little condo business to discuss. In fact, the only item on the agenda was the question of getting the eavestroughs cleaned so as to prevent last fall's clogged downspouts. Soon Vanessa was excusing herself to put the finishing touches on the main course.

∽◌◠◌∾

By the end of the meal, it was clear that Vanessa had come up with an inspired grouping of dishes for the first fall meeting of the Elderberry Gate Dinner Club.

"Vanessa and Gerald," said Todd, jumping to his feet, "that was a splendid meal to kick off our new season—fabulous food and wonderful wine. Let's raise our glasses in a toast everyone! To good times, good friends, and long lives!"

"And more chocolate tart!" said Nori. "That was awesome—absolutely the most silky chocolate taste ever."

"While we're busy congratulating ourselves, let's have a special round of applause for our rookie chef," said Vanessa. "Fiona—not only have you developed into an inspired lemon zester but now you tell me you have also become the proud possessor of a wire whisk. Anyone knows they can make a salad dressing by throwing the ingredients in a jar and then shaking the hell out of it, but Fiona is now a mistress of the art of emulsification."

"Thanks, guys," said Fiona, with a triumphant grin. "I'm feeling a bit like a kid right now. So many new things to try and now that I'm retired, so much time to try them in!"

"Wish I could say the same," said Nori. "Running the store seems to take all my energy and Todd is off on a buying trip next week. We have a list of 'Things To Do' that gets longer day by day."

Vanessa came in from the kitchen with fresh coffee. "It's a funny thing, though, how the things that you keep putting off sometimes turn out to be much more manageable than you ever imagined. Gerald and I had put off dealing with our wills, and you know how something like that can bother you. Well, we finally sat down to discuss them with our lawyer this week.

They're not totally settled yet because there's a few things we want to think about some more, but really, the whole thing was pretty painless."

There was a sudden hush at the table.

"Looks like you hit a nerve," said Gerald as he removed the glass stopper from a decanter of port. "Here we were, thinking we're the only people in the world disorganized enough not to have our wills in order. Now I'm not so sure we were alone."

"I wrote my will years ago, leaving everything to my parents," said Fiona. "With my mother gone, Dad's the sole beneficiary. Up to now, he's been pretty wealthy, but you never know. In the normal course of events, he's going to die before me and my will should take that into account."

"H'mm… I can see that could be a problem," said Nori. "But at least you're a step further along than we are. Because Todd and I have never legally married, we've sort of avoided all the other stuff, like making wills. But it really is crazy to keep our heads in the sand. If something happened to you, Todd, do we even know what would happen to the house and the other things we own?"

"Well, nothing's going to happen to me."

"But what if you got knocked down by a bus or got killed in a plane crash?"

"Gee, this is turning into a real cheerful conversation, isn't it? Doesn't anyone have any happy stories?"

"I guess our son would be pretty happy with the way our will stands," said Sheila. "After Jason was born, Doug and I bought one of those will kits and drew up our own wills. I think most things are still pretty much in order. The only foolish thing we did was to allow Jason to inherit everything at the age of 21. He's 18 now and I don't think he's suddenly going to get mature in three short years. We should have set up a trust to age 25 or so— maybe even 30! The idea that he could run through our hard-earned money in a few months buying stereo equipment, a fast car, and computer games is pretty scary."

"Come on, Sheila. You're selling him short," said Doug. "I'm sure we could rely on him to make a wise investment in a few hundred cases of beer as well!"

"Let's make a pact," said Vanessa. "Let's promise that by our November meeting, all of us will have at least spoken with our lawyers. Then we'll really have something to celebrate!"

DO I REALLY NEED A *Will?*

LET'S REVISIT THE SEPTEMBER GATHERING OF THE ELDERBERRY GATE DINNER CLUB. A delicious meal, good wine, convivial chat—but a hush fell over the dinner table when Vanessa mentioned that she and Gerald had been putting off their wills. Why should this be? For one thing, we don't like to talk about death much, and certainly making wills or talking about wills forces us to acknowledge our certain deaths. But also, as it turned out, each of the dinner club members had one or two "little" complexities in their will planning, just enough to deter them from getting to work on their wills—at least, "right now."

Gerald and *Vanessa* are a classic case: married later in life for a second time, each with adult children from a previous union.

Then there is *Fiona*—always career-focused and ambitious, Fiona never married and now faces the dilemma of where her estate should go, and whom she should ask to be her executor.

Todd and *Nori* present a modern challenge—happily partnered in work and in life, but not legally married, their independent attitudes have thus far stopped them from thinking about what would happen if either of them died.

And finally, there are ***Doug*** and ***Sheila***, only ever married to each other, their estate planning should be a breeze—but for that nagging concern that their son might soon squander any inheritance that came his way!

Let's have a look at these issues, all of which are quite common.

THE SECOND MARRIAGE

To get right to the nut, a second marriage gives rise to complexities in estate planning because of the children from a previous marriage of either or both partners.

Just like parents-in-law, people don't marry their stepchildren—stepchildren just come along with the new spouse, for better or worse. In the best case, the relationship between the child and step-parent is loving and cordial, but the step-parent may still be reluctant to treat his or her spouse's child as next of kin—especially if the step-parent also has children from a previous marriage. Not surprisingly, the means of including both the children and the second spouse in an estate plan raises several questions:

- First, will the children from previous marriages be included in the administration of their deceased parents' estates, as executors? If there are children on both sides, can they work well together, or should they be involved only in their own parent's estate? Can the children work with the surviving step-parent?

- Will the children receive all or part of their parent's estate? If so, what will the surviving second spouse receive? Will the distribution of personal items cause disagreement—items that the second spouse may feel belong to him or her now, but that the children remember fondly from their childhood?

- If, as Gerald and Vanessa are contemplating, a trust is set up for the lifetime of the surviving spouse, with the assets remaining after the surviving spouse's death going to the children of the first marriage, who will be the trustee of such a trust? Does it make sense to have the surviving spouse as the sole trustee (or even a co-trustee), when he or she is also a beneficiary of the trust as long as he or she lives?

- If the children from either of the first marriages are young enough to require a guardian, whom should that be? The fact that the first marriage ended may or may not indicate animosity between the parents—but if the second marriage results in children too, those children will be half siblings of the children from the first marriages, and, well, you can see how even the "simple" point of guardianship can give you a headache.

Planning as a Single Person

It's tempting to dismiss estate planning concerns for a single person like Fiona as trivial. After all, someone like Fiona likely has lots of money and so it should be an enviably easy task to divide it up!

Several issues arise, however, not least of which is deciding who should be the executor.

- Naming a parent may be a good idea during one's youth, but as the years go by, as Fiona is seeing, parents age and it becomes impractical to name them as executors.

- Similarly, naming a friend or colleague loses its appeal over time as everyone in that peer group begins to age.

- Common possibilities include a younger relative (a niece or nephew), or a corporate executor such as a trust company.

There is also the question of how to divide the estate up. Again, early in adulthood, it makes sense for a single person to leave it all to Mom and Dad, but as parents age, often they have more than enough resources of their own. The question then arises as to whether Mom and Dad can even look after their own estates, without adding more funds from a child's estate.

If that is the case, a child leaving all or part of an estate to aging parents may choose to set up a trust in his or her will. If the child dies before the parents, the child's estate will hold the funds in trust so that the parents' care can be paid for in the years ahead.

As well, people who are not married and do not have children often look at leaving substantial gifts to schools from which they graduated, the place of worship they attended, or a favourite arts group or charity.

COMMON-LAW RELATIONSHIPS

Here's a real minefield. After the myth of the simple will comes the myth of the "common-law" relationship. Who coined that phrase anyway? It implies a legal substance to the relationship that is not there—or at least wasn't there until the courts and governments began intervening some years ago. Since that intervention, in certain situations, a common-law relationship, or cohabitation, will be deemed to look sufficiently like a marriage to warrant the same legal treatment. Without getting into the moral debate as to whether that makes sense, the important point for estate planning is to be aware that the law in this area is a patchwork across Canada! It really comes down to not leaving one's affairs to be dealt with by the random application of the law on common-law unions. There's clearly a need to address both the possibility of a break-up with an unmarried partner and the inevitability of death.

Having said that, however, the approach of Nori and Todd is not uncommon. They had enough foresight to draw up a business agreement to cover their ownership of the store, but they haven't yet addressed their wills. Some questions to consider:

- Has either partner been married? If so, have all the property distribution issues been worked out, including the all-important division of pensions? If not, family relief legislation across Canada will require the parties to address their legal claims on the estates.

- Does either partner have children from another relationship? Again, those children must be considered in the estate plan.

- Do the partners want to treat each other "like spouses" and leave everything to each other, or are there parents and/or siblings to be looked after first? Take a look at how existing assets are held. For example, if a house was purchased together as "joint tenants," then the partners' wills won't have any effect on the house's disposition in the event of death— the surviving person is going to take over the entire house automatically because of the joint tenancy.

THE RED CORVETTE PROBLEM

Doug and Sheila of the Elderberry Gate Dinner Club seem quite "normal"—surely they will have "simple wills." They are even proud of the fact they did their own wills on a stationer's form many years ago!

However, Doug and Sheila have a gnawing concern that their son, Jason, spends money like a typical teenager, and the thought of him receiving their entire wealth anytime soon is a scary one! With a concern like this, the estate planning question really comes down to how much time and effort you want to invest in exploring the issues and the available options. For example, in Doug and Sheila's case, many options are open to them:

- They may conclude that life is short, they will be dead anyway, and leave it the way it is!

- Doug and Sheila could also look at the tax advantages of a trust, not only for their son, but also for their future grandchildren.

- They could describe in some detail the types of educational and medical distributions that the trustee can make to their son, and specify that other distributions be simply based on his age.

- Regarding who will administer their estate, Doug and Sheila could look at all sorts of options for the trustee: a close friend, a relative, a trusted adviser, or a corporate executor.

So, in summary, what is the best way of getting started on this tricky task of estate planning? Vanessa's idea of having an informal chat with a lawyer friend is quite good —at least it gets the creative juices going. It's also helpful to share the process with friends, the way Vanessa and Gerald did with the Elderberry Gate Dinner Club, because one thing soon becomes very clear—most people are in the same boat! Finally, there is a lot to be said for setting a goal for when to have things resolved, and don't forget about also planning a reward—like a great meal with good friends!

THE *Menu*

⋘⋙

Potted goat's cheese with Pita Chips

Roasted pork tenderloin with curried apples and currants

Mesclun salad with a lemon shallot vinaigrette

Wilted kale with roasted garlic

Toasted almond bulgur

Chocolate Chantilly tart with a butter pastry

⋘⋙

Potted goat's cheese with Pita Chips   SERVES 8

This is a very easy, yet impressive appetizer and can be made a day or two ahead. Serve it with pita chips or a very simple cracker, such as a water cracker. As it is quite rich, it is not well suited to a buttery cracker or pastry. Another alternative is to spread it on flour tortillas with a bit of mesclun greens, roll the tortillas into cylinders, and slice diagonally into ½-inch (1 cm) slices.

8 ounces	soft goat's cheese	250 g
2 tbsp.	chopped pistachios*	25 mL
2 tbsp.	coarsely chopped dried cranberries	25 mL
1 tbsp.	coarsely chopped black olives	15 mL
	grated zest from ½ fresh lemon	
1 tbsp.	chopped fresh basil	15 ml
1 clove	garlic, minced	1 clove
1 tbsp.	balsamic vinegar	15 mL
2 tbsp.	extra virgin olive oil	25 mL
1 tsp.	smooth Dijon mustard	5 mL
	salt and pepper, to taste	

* Use toasted pine nuts if you prefer.

1. Gently mix together the goat's cheese, pistachios, dried cranberries, olives, and lemon zest.

2. In a separate bowl, whisk together the basil, garlic, balsamic vinegar, olive oil, Dijon mustard, and salt and pepper.

3. Pour the oil and vinegar mixture over the goat's cheese mixture and mix until barely blended. Some of the vinaigrette should remain separate from the goat's cheese.

4. Transfer the cheese to a decorative crock or bowl, cover with plastic wrap, and refrigerate for at least one hour. Bring to room temperature before serving.

Pita chips   SERVES 6 TO 8

6-inch (15 cm) pita breads
Extra virgin olive oil in a spray bottle or atomizer
Dried oregano
Salt
Freshly ground black pepper

1. Heat oven to 400°F (200°C). Cut each pita round in half, then each semicircle into five wedges. (If the brand of pita bread you are using is very thick, split each one in half horizontally before cutting it into wedges.)

2. Spread the pita wedges in a single layer on two or three baking sheets. Spray the wedges lightly with olive oil (or dab with a pastry brush dipped in olive oil). Sprinkle them with dried oregano, salt and pepper. Bake until lightly browned and crisp. Cool and serve.

Roasted pork tenderloin with curried apples and currants SERVES 8

Pork should be served to a medium degree of doneness—just pale pink. Contrary to the belief with which you probably grew up, pork, at least in Canada, no longer contains trichinosis.

1 tbsp.	butter	15 mL
1 tbsp.	canola oil	15 mL
4	whole pork tenderloins	4
	(8 to 10 ounces/250 to 280g each)	
4	firm fleshed apples,	4
	such as Granny Smith or Gala,	
	cut into ¼ inch (5 mm) thick slices	
½	large onion, cut into small dice	½
4 tsp.	Madras curry paste	20 mL
¼ tsp.	cinnamon	1 ml
¼ tsp.	ground coriander	1 mL
2 cloves	garlic, minced	2 cloves
1 inch piece	fresh ginger, peeled and grated	2.5 cm piece
⅓ cup	dry white wine	75 mL
1 tbsp.	cider vinegar	15 mL
¼ cup	dried currants*	50 mL
1 cup	heavy cream (35 % M.F.)	250 mL
2 tsp.	chopped coriander or parsley	10 mL
	salt and white pepper, to taste	

* It's best to use fresh, soft currants, but if all you have are hard, dry pellets, soak them in very hot (boiled, but not boiling) water for five minutes. Add a little brandy to the water, if you have it.

1. Heat oven to 375°F (190°C).

2. On high heat, heat butter and canola oil in a large skillet or frying pan until almost smoking. Add pork tenderloins and season them with salt and black pepper, reducing the heat when the oil begins to smoke. Using tongs, turn them several times until they are brown on all sides. Do not pierce with a fork, as this will cause the juice to run from the meat.

3. Remove the pan from the heat. Remove the meat from the pan and place it on a baking sheet or in a low-sided roasting pan. Put it into the oven and roast for approximately 20 minutes. Prepare the sauce while the meat cooks.

4. Sauce: In the skillet used to brown the meat, cook the apples and onion over medium-high heat until golden brown and softened.

5. Add the curry paste, cinnamon, coriander, garlic, and fresh ginger. Cook until fragrant, approximately 1 minute.

6. Deglaze the pan with white wine, scraping up the bits of browned meat and spices. Cook for an additional 1 minute. (During this time, the volume of the wine should decrease by about one-half.) Add the cider vinegar.

7. Add the currants and cream, and reduce volume by one-half, stirring frequently. Add cilantro or parsley. Remove the pan from the heat.

8. Season with salt and white pepper. The sauce should be sweet, spicy, very flavourful, rich, and a bit tart. If the apples and currants do not impart enough sweetness for your taste, whisk in a little apple juice, 1 tablespoon (15 mL) at a time.

9. Test the meat for doneness by inserting an instant-read thermometer *
¾-inch (2 cm) into the thickest part of the roast. When it reads 140°F
(60°C), remove the tenderloin from the oven and allow it to sit at
room temperature for 10 minutes.

10. Slice the meat on the diagonal into ½ inch (1 cm) thick medallions.
Reheat the sauce, pour it on a platter, and arrange the pork medallions
on top.

* If you don't have an instant-read thermometer, test doneness like this:
Hold out one hand, palm up. With the middle finger of the opposite
hand, feel the fleshy part of the palm, in the area below the thumb. This
is how the meat will feel when it is raw. Now make a tight fist and feel the
same area. This is how the meat will feel when it is well done. What you
are looking for is something approximately halfway in between.

Mesclun salad with a lemon shallot vinaigrette   SERVES 8

3	shallots, peeled and thinly sliced	3
1 tbsp.	olive oil	15 ml
	Grated zest from ½ fresh lemon	
1 tbsp.	fresh lemon juice	15 mL
4 tbsp.	red wine vinegar	20 mL
1 tsp.	dry mustard	5 mL
¼ tsp.	sugar	1 mL
¾ cup	extra virgin olive oil	175 ml
1 tsp.	chopped, fresh, mild herb,	5 ml
	such as parsley, basil, or chervil	
	Salt and black pepper, to taste	
8 ounces	mesclun greens	250 g

1. Sauté the shallots in 1 tablespoon (15 mL) of olive oil, over medium-high heat, until golden, soft, and lightly browned. Allow to cool to room temperature.

2. In a bowl, whisk together the shallots, lemon zest, lemon juice, vinegar, mustard, and sugar.

3. Whisking constantly, slowly add the olive oil in a thin, steady stream.

4. Whisk in chopped herbs. Season with salt and pepper.

5. Immediately before serving, toss the greens with approximately ¼ cup (50 mL) of vinaigrette. (Begin with ⅛ cup (25 mL), and add more, as needed. Do not overdress the greens.) Save the remaining vinaigrette to dress grilled fish or chicken breast, sautéed zucchini, roasted pork loin, or salad.

Wilted kale with roasted garlic

SERVES 8

Green kale is a dark, curly, somewhat peppery winter green, rich in potassium and vitamin A. For this menu, do not substitute decorative purple or white kale, as both are tougher and have a more pronounced, cabbage-like taste. Instead, use Swiss chard, if need be.

1 whole bulb	garlic	1 whole bulb
2 tbsp.	olive oil	25 mL
3 bunches	green kale, washed, dried, and coarsely chopped	3 bunches
	Salt and black pepper, to taste	

1. Heat oven or toaster oven to 325°F (160°C).

2. Place the garlic on a double thickness of aluminum foil, approximately 8 inches (20 cm) square. Drizzle 1 teaspoon (5 mL) olive oil on the bulb. Form a loose tent with the foil, and seal tightly.

3. Roast the garlic for 1 hour, until it is golden brown and soft. Set it aside to cool. (Garlic may be roasted one day ahead, and refrigerated in plastic wrap. Do not store in foil, as the garlic will become discoloured. Be generous with the plastic wrap, for obvious reasons!)

4. When it is cool enough to handle, flip the garlic bulb over, and using a serrated knife, slice off the bottom of the bulb. Squeeze the softened cloves into a small bowl, and mash them slightly with a fork.

5. Heat the remaining olive oil in a skillet over medium-high heat.

6. When the oil is very hot, add the kale to the pan, all at once, and stir.

7. Add half the garlic, breaking it down and working it into the kale with a wooden spoon.

8. Continue to cook, stirring frequently until the kale is wilted, but not soft, approximately 5 minutes. Season with salt and pepper.

Toasted almond bulgur

SERVES 8

If you are unable to find bulgur at your grocery store, look for cracked wheat in the cereal aisle.

1½ cups	water or chicken stock	375 mL
1½ cups	bulgur	375 mL
⅓ cup	sliced, unblanched almonds	75 mL
1 tbsp.	chopped flat leaf parsley	15 mL

1. Heat the oven to 350°F (180°C).

2. In a skillet or sauté pan, bring the liquid to a boil. Add the bulgur and stir. Turn off the heat, cover, and let stand until all the moisture is absorbed.

3. Spread the almonds on a baking sheet and toast in the oven for 6 to 8 minutes, until they are brown. Turn the nuts out onto a cutting board immediately.

4. Coarsely crush the toasted nuts by lightly rolling them with a rolling pin. (For convenience, put the toasted almonds into a clean bag before rolling.)

5. Stir the nuts into the bulgur. Add the parsley, and season with salt and pepper.

Chocolate Chantilly tart with a butter pastry   SERVES 8 TO 12

Butter pastry

½ cup	butter, at room temperature	125 mL
½ cup	superfine (berry) sugar	125 mL
½ tsp.	vanilla extract	2 mL
1 cup	all-purpose flour	250 mL
	pinch of salt	

1. Heat the oven to 375°F (190°C).

2. With an electric mixer, cream together the butter and sugar until well blended, but not fluffy.

3. Add the vanilla, mixing to combine.

4. Add the flour and salt. Mix to form a soft dough.

5. Pat the dough into a 10-inch (25 cm) tart pan with a removable base.

6. Bake until golden, approximately 20 minutes. At this point, it isn't necessary to cool the shell.

Chocolate ganache

2 ounces	dark chocolate (remember the chocolate rule—use the best you can afford)	50 g
3 tbsp.	heavy cream (35% M.F.)	50 ml

1. Put the dark chocolate and cream in a glass or ceramic bowl. Microwave on medium until most of the chocolate is melted.

2. Remove the bowl from the microwave and stir the mixture until completely melted.

3. Pour the chocolate into the pastry shell. Spread it with a pastry brush or the back of a spoon. Allow the pastry shell and the chocolate ganache to cool, completely.

Chocolate Chantilly filling

2 cups plus ½ cup	milk (not low fat)	500mL plus 125 mL
4	egg yolks	4
⅔ cup	sugar	150 mL
⅓ cup	corn starch	75 mL
¼ cup	Dutch processed cocoa powder	50 mL
6 ounces	dark chocolate, chopped	170g
2 tbsp.	butter	25 mL
1 tsp.	vanilla extract	5 mL
¾cup	heavy cream (35% M.F.)	175 mL

1. In a heavy saucepan, over medium-high heat, scald 2 cups (500 mL) milk (heat until very hot, but not boiling).

2. In a large bowl, using a wire whisk, beat together the ½ cup milk (125 mL), egg yolks, sugar, corn starch, and cocoa powder.

3. Pour one-third of the scalded milk into the egg yolks, whisking gently. (This is called tempering, and prevents the eggs from cooking too quickly and "curdling" the sauce.) Add the egg mixture back into scalded milk, and gently stir over medium-low heat until the custard is the consistency of pudding.

4. Remove the mixture from the heat. Strain it into a bowl, and stir in the chocolate, butter, and vanilla. Chill for at least 3 hours.

5. Once the chocolate mixture has chilled, whip the cream to soft peaks.

6. Remove the chocolate mixture from the refrigerator and whip it until it is soft and lump free. Mix one-third of the whipped cream into the chocolate mixture to lighten it, then gently fold in the remainder of the cream.

7. Pour the chocolate filling into the cooled pastry shell.

8. Chill at least 3 hours.

To finish the tart:

¾ cup	heavy cream (35% M.F.)	175 mL
1 tbsp.	icing sugar	15 mL
½ tsp.	vanilla	2 mL

1. Whip the cream, icing sugar, and vanilla extract until firm but not have stiff peaks form when the whisk is lifted from the cream. Spread on the top of the tart.

To decorate the tart (optional):

Drizzle additional cooled chocolate ganache in a random pattern across the top of the finished tart.

Or:

Slightly warm a small block of dark chocolate in the microwave oven, on defrost, for 15 to 20 seconds. Grate it with a cheese grater or a vegetable peeler directly onto the tart. Repeat with milk chocolate.

Advance preparation

The day before the dinner:

Make the potted goat's cheese and Chocolate Chantilly tart.

The day of the dinner:

A.M.

Make the lemon shallot vinaigrette, roast the garlic, wash and chop the kale, and toast the almonds.

P.M.

Slice the apples and toss them in lemon juice or cider vinegar to prevent them from browning. Measure and prepare all ingredients for the pork tenderloin and place them in a convenient spot beside the stove, except for the cream and pork, which should be refrigerated.

Shortly before the guests arrive

Allow the potted goat's cheese to sit at room temperature for about one hour.

FESTIVE *Seafood* DINNER

FIONA WOKE TO THE SOUND OF FREEZING RAIN RATTLING AGAINST HER BEDROOM WINDOW. Pulling aside the curtain, she found the downtown towers of glass and steel were transformed into ghostly apparitions, their tops lost in a heavy pall of grey cloud. Being retired had been fun in the summer; perhaps even better was the freedom to stay cozy under her duvet while others, less fortunate, did battle with frosted windshields and gusty winds.

Snuggling down in the warmth of her bed, Fiona prepared to doze off again —all to no avail. After a lifetime of jumping out of bed at the first buzz of the alarm, Fiona was finding that her body was programmed to want to get up and at it even when she no longer knew what "it" was. She reached for her appointment calendar, which, by force of habit, she still kept on her bedside table. Looking at the week ahead, the clear expanses of white space seemed both an opportunity and a reproof. Fiona was troubled by the fact that since she had retired she was finding that one day seemed to slide into the next.

Most of the exciting things she had looked forward to achieving had not yet been put into place. "Oh, come on, Fee," she said out loud, the sound of her voice at odds with the quiet of the room. "Don't be so hard on yourself!" And indeed, when she took stock, it wasn't all bad—in her

first spring and summer off, she'd planted window boxes and patio tomatoes, researched a trip to Tuscany, signed up for Italian lessons, and taken
her dad to visit relatives in Saskatchewan. Heck, she'd even organized her
sock drawer!

What she hadn't done, she thought with a sinking heart, was to buy
some dining room chairs. A few years ago, a friend had invited her to go
to an auction and at some point during the proceedings she found herself
the proud owner of a heavy oak refectory table. In the ensuing days, Fiona
thought that some kind of madness must have overcome her. Why on
earth had she thought she needed a large dining room table, when she
never entertained? Last year, when it had been her turn to host the
Elderberry Gate Dinner Club, she had uncovered it, almost with delight,
from under a thick sediment of seismic charts and annual reports. Of
course, she had had to ask her neighbours to bring their own chairs saying airily, "This time, next year, I'll be retired and I will have tracked down
the perfect chairs to match my table!" Now it was her turn to host again
and all she had were a couple of dated kitchen chairs—hand-me-downs
from the sale of her parents' home. "Oh, well, Dad has taken up a lot of
my time," she thought, and as if on cue, the telephone rang.

"Hi, Dad—funny, I was just thinking about you. What do you mean,
can I come and get you?"

"Well, I don't know how else I can get down to the office. Someone
seems to have driven off with my car during the night. My briefcase has van-
ished, too! I don't know if this is someone's idea of a joke but *I* don't find it
the slightest bit funny."

Fiona felt a prickly rush of panic. During their long drive to
Saskatchewan, there had been times when her dad had come out with
some rather strange utterances but nothing like this.

"Hey, Dad," she said in a voice she hoped was light, yet controlled.
"Nice way to try and get me out of bed in the morning. Did you think I'd

forgotten you're retired from Pioneer Insurance? It's got to be more than 15 years!"

"But Fee, what about my car? I guess I should call the police and get them onto it right away. They say there are gangs at work that can strip..."

"Dad, please don't call the police," Fiona interrupted. "Remember we sold your car—it was when you decided to move into the Lodge. Remember how we worked out how many taxis you could take in a year and not come even close to the cost of operating and insuring the Buick?"

Fiona certainly remembered the scene sitting at her parents' kitchen table—receipts and statements from the car dealer and the insurance company all neatly bundled and itemized, her dad at age 82 whizzing through the mental arithmetic with his customary disdain for a calculator or any other kind of "cheat machine." And how sensible and rational he'd been about the whole business! The Buick dated back to the time when Fiona's mother had been alive so he must have felt some emotional attachment to it. But once he'd figured out the economics of the situation, he'd cheerfully sold the car to a young couple without a murmur of regret.

"Don't be ridiculous, Fiona," said her dad, his voice rising in annoyance. "Don't you think I'd remember selling my own car? I may be getting on but I'm not stupid!"

No, thought Fiona sadly. Not stupid, but probably sick. "Give me a few minutes to get some clothes on, Dad. I'll be over as soon as I can— just promise me you won't call the police!"

⁓◌◠◌⁓

Returning to her home two hours later, Fiona thought back with longing to the blissful sense of ignorance with which she had started the day. "You just never know what's around the corner," she muttered to herself as she straightened the covers on the bed she'd abandoned so hastily. Seeing her dad agitated and acting totally out of character had been bad enough; worse was finding out this was only the latest in a string of similar incidents. What was it that the Lodge administrator had said? "We've had your father under observation for a while now. Of course, we never want to act precipitately and Mr. McCarthy has been one of our model residents but when it comes to the safety and comfort of the other residents…" Just how bad had it been, Fiona had wanted to know, and then wished she hadn't asked. "Well, the most disturbing incident was last Thursday when your father approached Mr. Heinrich and asked him to stop whistling. When he didn't stop right away, your father gave him a shove and before we knew it there was a scuffle going on in the middle of the Activity Room."

The news was almost more than Fiona could bear. Her own sweet dad, always the perfect gentleman, actually roughing up an 85-year-old man pushing a walker! And what seemed even more amazing was that Fiona had picked him up for his monthly blood work later that very day and he'd seemed absolutely fine. In fact, while they were sitting in the waiting room at the lab, he'd kept her entertained with a wonderful string of reminiscences about his early life in the Scottish highlands. Sadly, however, she could only agree that her dad's current medical condition needed to be assessed. The words of the Lodge administrator had summed it all up very succinctly—"Of course, I'm no expert, but based on past experience, your father seems to be exhibiting some of the classic signs of Alzheimer's disease. We'll likely need to get him referred to a chronic care facility—as you know, the Lodge is not set up to provide the kind of attention he'll need. You can rest assured we'll do everything we can to help."

Over the next two weeks, "resting assured" was one of the few things that Fiona did *not* do. Being an only child, she found herself dwelling on the state of her father's sickness almost to the exclusion of everything else. She hadn't realized how much she had isolated herself until she ran into Vanessa one afternoon on the front steps.

"Fiona! Where have you been hiding yourself? You're not that worried about hosting our November dinner, are you?"

Fiona could only mumble a few words in response before collapsing into tears.

"Fee—for heaven's sake, girl! You'd better come in and tell me what this is all about."

Sitting in Vanessa's kitchen, Fiona felt grateful to be sharing the burden of grief she had been carrying around for days.

"I just can't get over how quickly he's deteriorating. Last week I sat in on a session where this young doctor asked Dad a whole bunch of questions—the sort of things he would have scoffed at as unworthy of an answer just a month or so ago."

"What kind of questions?" asked Vanessa.

"Oh, you know the kind of thing—'What's the date today?' and 'What's your address?' Dad was a bit mixed up but with a little prompting he eventually came up with the right answers. Then the doctor asked Dad the name of the current prime minister. I thought now we're in for it—Dad has some very definite views on Chrétien. I'd heard about them at length on our trip to Saskatchewan! So what does Dad say? 'Oh, that's an easy one. Good old Dief—we finally got a Prairie boy in Ottawa.' I tell you, Vanessa, I had a hard time not bursting into tears."

"It must be so difficult when someone you've respected and loved your whole life through suddenly becomes a stranger."

"That's exactly it," said Fiona. "When the diagnosis was confirmed as Alzheimer's, I looked at the person who seemed to be occupying my dad's body and I felt like shouting 'Get out of there, you imposter. I want my dad back!' I can't believe how childish *I'm* being."

"It happens to all of us," said Vanessa with a wry smile. "When my mother died four years ago I felt utterly abandoned. Imagine the foolishness of it—me a grown woman in my fifties feeling like I'd been orphaned! Your situation is probably worse—it would be dreadful if your dad didn't recognize you."

"Yes. I'd been thinking that things couldn't be so bad if Dad still knew who I was, but during my last visit, he called me Vera a couple of times—Vera's my mother's name."

"Oh, Fiona—I'm so sorry. You'll just have to try very hard to remember all the good times you've had with him. Put those memories away somewhere safe and don't let what you're going through right now affect them. What does he think about moving to a nursing home?"

"Not too many objections so far—although it's hard to figure out the way his mind is working these days. The other night the porter discovered my dad trying to walk out the front door in his pyjamas so it's clear he can't stay at the Lodge much longer. They're keeping a close eye on him but I'll be glad to have him settled in a place with 24-hour supervision. It shouldn't be too long now."

"Well, at least you'll be able to relax a bit, knowing he's in a safe environment and that he's being well cared for. You can't help your dad any by worrying over him so you might as well get on with your own life, hard as that might seem right now."

"I guess you're right. I've really let everything slide, especially the fact that I'm supposed to be hosting our November dinner club meeting in less than a week and I haven't done a thing about it!"

"Hey, that's no problem. We'd all completely understand if you cancelled."

"No, I'd like to go ahead with it. It would be nice to be thinking of something other than my dad taking pot shots at old guys who whistle! Do you think you could help me pull it off, Vanessa?"

"It's as good as done, Fee. Or at least it will be just as soon as we have ourselves a glass of wine. You start looking through that stack of food magazines and I'll dig out a bottle. A nice glass of Merlot will be just what the doctor ordered!"

⸎

The next morning, Fiona was pleased to find herself getting up with a sense of anticipation rather than despair. Vanessa was right—there was absolutely no point in continuing to worry about her dad. They'd been promised the next available nursing home bed, and while there was some hope that medication might slow down the progression of his condition, there was nothing anyone could do to return him to his previous state. In the meantime, she should stop feeling sorry for herself. After all, she was in an enviable position—a single woman with all the time in the world, plenty of money (bolstered by a generous stock pay-out), good health, and a keen desire to try all the things she had denied herself through her hectic days in the oilpatch.

"*Va bene*," she remembered from her Italian class. "*Molto bene!*"

Putting a menu together with Vanessa's help had been fairly simple and actually lots of fun. Vanessa had suggested that seafood would be a good theme to build the meal around. "In the old days, before proper refrigeration, they used to say you could only serve seafood if there was an 'r' in the month, which, of course, eliminated the summer months of May through August. Nowadays, they're farmed year round but I still think that seafood tastes better in the winter."

Fiona finally settled on a dish of saffron wild rice pilaf with prawns, chorizo, sweet peppers, and corn. "Good choice," Vanessa had said approvingly. "The chorizo sausage will spice it up and make the expensive prawns stretch a bit further. It's also great to have a one-dish meal like that when you're entertaining."

Fiona certainly hoped so. The magazine showed a picture of a relaxed hostess, dressed in silk, serving perfectly composed portions of pilaf on Portugese hand-painted plates. To add further insult, the guests were happily seated on lovely old antique chairs that, by rights, should have been in Fiona's own dining room!

Vanessa had offered to bring an appetizer course of fresh oysters and together they'd decided that the Enrights could be asked to bring a salad and bread to round out the meal. "Why don't you ask Todd and Nori to bring a dessert of their choice?" Vanessa had suggested. "I'm sure they'll come up with something special. Maybe it could have a Christmas theme since we won't have a dinner club meeting in December."

The mention of Christmas had awakened some painful thoughts in Fiona's mind—thoughts that had stayed with her after she had left the warmth of Vanessa's kitchen and returned home alone. Since her mom had died, Fiona and her dad had established a new tradition of going through their stockings together on Christmas morning over hot chocolate and cranberry muffins. The contents of her stocking were always the same—a gift certificate for books, a pair of size 7 ½ black leather gloves, and a box of chocolate-covered almonds—but her dad's face never lost its expression of excited anticipation as she withdrew each item. "Is it what you want, dear?" he would always say. "I do hope so."

"Dear old dad," said Fiona. "I miss you already."

⁓◌◌⁓

With only three days to go to the party, Fiona had resigned herself to the deficiencies in her dining room furniture. But now that the food plans were all in place, what was the harm in having a little prowl around a few antique stores, just on the off-chance? The first three stores had nothing suitable but in the fourth one, the owner's eyes lit up when she described what she was looking for. "How about these little beauties?" he had said with a flourish, pulling the dust cover off a stack of six Sheraton-style chairs upholstered in flaming orange shiny polyester. "I've been meaning to get them recovered—that colour seems to put a lot of people off."

"No kidding," said Fiona. "Would you throw in a pair of sunglasses as part of the deal?"

"They're actually damn good chairs—solid construction, and they've all been re-glued. That's the trouble with half the stuff that's shipped here in containers—a couple of months in this dry climate, the wood shrinks and stuff starts to fall apart. We wait 'til they've acclimatized, then take them apart and re-glue them. These chairs are over a hundred years old from Scotland and they've been fitted back together like new!"

"Scotland?" said Fiona. "That's where my parents came from."

"Imagine that! These could have been your granny's chairs, then," said the owner.

"Well, if they were, she would never have covered them in that colour of fabric."

"Course she wouldn't have, love. Some bright spark must have done that thinking it would make them more saleable. It's easy enough to change— a couple of metres of fabric would do it."

"Well, I might have been interested, but you see I've got this enormous table and I really wanted to get eight chairs. You've only got six here."

"This has got to be your lucky day! Most people don't want eight so I was thinking of breaking up the set and selling the two armchairs as a pair. Easiest thing in the world to bring 'em up from the basement!"

⸎

Fiona was happy that the antique store's delivery truck arrived mid-morning when none of the other residents were around. She had slipped a note in each mailbox saying, "No need to bring chairs, after all!" but she still wanted the final effect to be a surprise.

On the advice of her new friend in the antiques business, Fiona had rented a power stapler and had purchased some tightly woven fabric to recover the seats. "Jacquard," the woman in the fabric store had called it and the colour—a rich claret—seemed to perfectly match this lovely name. The first chair took her some time, especially learning how to stretch the fabric completely taut, but by the end of the day she had finished the lot. What a transformation! The patina of the old wood and the ruby richness of the upholstery magically warmed the tan walls of the room. Almost giddy with success, Fiona stood back to admire her achievement. Now she couldn't wait to put together the finishing touches.

∽◎◎∽

"Ten minutes to blastoff," thought Fiona, "and all systems *go*!" She was so excited—to think that her dining room could look like something you might see in a magazine! The new place mats had been somewhat of an extravagance—but how could she have resisted? Made of a warm gold brocade and trimmed with a silken cord, they formed a perfect foil against the dark oak of the table. She'd set a twinkling tea light at each person's place and then grouped ivory candles at each end of the table. And just wait until Nori took a look at her centrepiece! Fiona had used her mother's pressed-glass stand as the base for a pyramid of persimmons and pomegranates interspersed with fragrant fresh bay leaves.

The next moment, her newfound cockiness evaporated into thin air as she realized she had left all the price tags on the new white linen napkins. And when the doorbell rang, Fiona greeted her guests with an armful of napkins and so many tags stuck to her fingers that she couldn't shake hands with anyone.

"Hi guys," said Fiona. "I was just pretending to be organized."

∽◎◎∽

"Your fingers may be tacky but your dining room sure isn't!" exclaimed Sheila Enright. "This looks fabulous!"

"I love the centrepiece, Fiona. The colours are just perfect in this room," said Nori with genuine admiration.

"Centrepiece shmentrepiece! What I like is that there's finally something to sit on. Good job, Fiona—the chairs look great. Feel great, too!" said Todd as he tested one out. "So now you'll be able to have us over every night for dinner."

"Suits me," said Fiona. "Just as long as you guys bring over the food, you can come whenever you want. Oh, and speaking of food, Vanessa, where do you think we should serve the oysters?"

"Gerald has just taken them through to the kitchen. Is that okay? I wouldn't want any of the ice dripping on your coffee table."

✸

As the group stood around the kitchen island devouring the oysters, Doug reminded them of why they were gathering. "I've been asked to call this meeting to order," he said. "We do have the odd bit of condo business to discuss but we don't want to interfere with Fiona's dinner plans. How long do we have, Fee?"

"It doesn't really matter—just give me the five-minute warning so I can throw in the prawns. But I do have one small request. When the oysters are finished, would you be nice enough to move your business meeting into the living room? As a rookie chef, I feel kind of nervous with all of you looking on, especially if I'm going to do something brilliant like dumping the platter on the floor."

"Okay—we'll make sure to consult you if we make any momentous decisions about snow removal. And Sheila and I will need a few minutes, too, to put the salad together."

✸

After everyone enthusiastically tasted Fiona's saffron-hued prawn pilaf, Todd felt compelled to leap to his feet. "Let's have a toast to Fiona's wonderful new, or should I say old, chairs! And to her delicious pilaf with its perfectly cooked prawns, and to Doug and Sheila for their spectacular salad and fabulous focaccia. Long life to all!"

"After being with my dad this past month, I'd have to say, be careful what you wish for—it might come true," Fiona said ruefully.

"What do you mean?" asked Nori. "The last time I heard about your dad he was in great shape."

"Oh, he still is in great shape, physically. Old Scottish crofter stock, you know. It's his mind that's gone. On our trip in May he was figuring out exactly how many kilometres we were getting to the litre, now he can't remember what he ate for lunch two minutes ago."

As the guests expressed their concern and sympathy, Fiona hurried on.

"The good news is I just heard we can get him into a good nursing home next week. I'll be so relieved to have him settled. He loved being in the Lodge, thought the food was great, and he had his bridge buddies and lots of friends there but they're just not set up to provide full-time nursing care."

"From what I've heard about your dad, he must have put up quite a stink. How did you handle the subject of the move?" asked Todd.

"Luckily, he didn't seem to mind. I think the world of someone with Alzheimer's shrinks to a very small space. It's almost as if he's forgotten that he ever had any friends. But the thing is, I have to take charge of his life now. I'm just so thankful that when Dad was still in his right mind he had a personal directive drawn up authorizing me to make some decisions on his behalf."

"Does that include financial matters?"

"No—the way the lawyer described it, every individual has two components, at least as far as the law is concerned. There's the 'person,' which involves non-financial issues, and then there's the 'estate,' which is made up of assets and income and so on. Dad used an enduring power of attorney appointing me to take care of all his financial stuff when he was no longer able to do so—I think they call that a contingent power of attorney."

"Where does this personal directive thing come in?"

"When you draw up a personal directive, you're also appointing someone to make decisions on your behalf. But instead of finances, the directive deals with day-to-day issues such as health care and where you're
going to live. It also gives you the opportunity to state your beliefs on
things like life support. Dad had an older brother in Saskatchewan who
had liver cancer. In spite of a poor prognosis, some hotshot doctor insisted on putting him on an aggressive course of chemotherapy. Of course,
Uncle George died anyway, but not before going through a terrible time.
Dad was determined that would never happen to him."

"Is a personal directive the same as a living will?" asked Nori.

"Sort of," said Gerald. "Vanessa and I had quite a discussion with our
lawyer, Miriam Perlman, on that very issue. I had a living will drawn up
a number of years ago. Miriam explained that living wills had always been
in a kind of grey area—not exactly legally binding but certainly to be
taken into account. So provincial governments started bringing in legislation to correct the situation. Miriam strongly recommended that both
Vanessa and I should have a personal directive that clearly states our pref-
erences and would be legally binding."

"Yes," interrupted Vanessa. "I even stipulated that I wanted a good
haircut and a manicure every six weeks. Even if I'm not all there, I still
have my self-respect to consider."

"My dad's personal directive is pretty straightforward," said Fiona as
she cleared the table. "The great thing about it is that he trusts me to make
the right choices on his behalf although it does also spell out his views on
things like artificially prolonging his life and donating organs. I know I'm

probably going to have to make some hard decisions in the future but those decisions would be much harder if I didn't have this document to guide me."

Draining his wineglass, Todd asked, "So how is the personal directive helping you to arrange the move?"

"When all this trouble started, Dad was assessed by two doctors who both declared him 'mentally incompetent.' That was a pretty hard thing for me to hear—I've looked up to my dad my whole life, but you have to face reality. From that point on, I became legally authorized to make all the decisions about Dad's day-to-day living arrangements. It was apparent that he couldn't go on living at the Lodge and so with a clear conscience I could start making arrangements to get him moved to a nursing home."

"Sheila and I are thinking about what we want to put in our personal directives," said Doug. "Our lawyer suggested that when we get together to bring our will up to date we should also talk about a personal directive and an enduring power of attorney. I always thought that if you got your will done, you were laughing, but it seems it's a bit more complicated than that."

"Hm," said Vanessa. "I was wondering how everyone had made out on our pact to at least have spoken with our lawyers before this meeting. Should we break for dessert and then carry on this discussion over coffee?"

"Good idea," said Fiona. "I guess we'll need a big serving spoon. Nori, if you can get the dessert from the fridge, I'll grab the plates and forks. Shall we make Todd serve it?"

❧◉☙

When Nori presented the dessert, there were gratifying gasps of admiration. "Todd's a big fan of trifle," Nori said, "but we decided to create something with a more modern twist. This is made with hazelnut sponge cake and an orange mascarpone filling."

"M'mm … decadent," said Sheila, watching Todd spoon out generous helpings. For once, silence fell over the group as they each savoured the delicate combination of flavours.

❧◉☙

"Shall we take our coffee in the living room or do you want to stay here?" asked Fiona.

"Here is fine," said Sheila, looking around the table for consensus. "Your new chairs are so comfortable!"

"How did we all make out on our assignment?" asked Vanessa. "I can start by saying that Gerald and I got everything finalized since our last meeting. We now have shiny new wills, together with personal directives, *and* enduring powers of attorney! The funny thing is that getting everything taken care of has actually made me stop thinking about death."

"Vanessa—surely you weren't going around thinking about death all the time?" asked Gerald, looking at his wife with surprise.

"No, of course not. But you know how it is—you get on a plane and you think, I sure hope we don't crash because I've left my affairs in a bit of a mess and I didn't even get around to cleaning out the fridge or changing the cat litter."

"I know exactly where you're coming from," laughed Sheila. "Now that Doug and I have made an appointment with our lawyer, I can hardly wait to get it all tidied up so I don't have to worry about it anymore. And I think we've agreed to fix our will so that any money Jason inherits from us will be held in trust until he's 30. In his first semester at university, he's run up a phone bill of several hundred dollars—he just doesn't seem to have a concept of living within his means."

"Good for you. I bet you'll both be all done before you know it. Fiona—you've had a few other things to keep you busy this past month rather than thinking about your own affairs."

"Actually, I *have* been in touch with my lawyer. As my will stands right now, my dad receives everything outright, which doesn't make a lot of sense any more. I will probably outlive my dad so I've been thinking of some charities I'd like to support. The other thing I've been thinking about is whom I should name in my own personal directive. Without any siblings or kids, that's kind of a tricky one. I could ask one of my friends, I suppose, but they're all pretty much my age. I *do* have a god-daughter and I've been thinking of asking her, but I'm not sure how she would react."

"You've actually got quite a lot of stuff to think about before you meet with your lawyer again," Vanessa commented.

"At least you've got the time to think," said Nori. "I guess we need to fess up. Todd and I have been so busy getting the store ready for the holiday season that we haven't done a thing. Certainly, we won't have to worry about coming up with a New Year's resolution. We both know what we've got to do—now we just have to do it."

"Sounds like a Nike ad," said Sheila with a laugh. "I think we're meeting at your place in January, aren't we? We'll look forward to an update then."

"And in the meantime," said Gerald, standing, "I hope that everyone has a very happy holiday and a prosperous and healthy New Year!"

FACING *Incompetency* HEAD-ON

November's dinner party raises the unsettling challenge fac-
ing most of us at some time or another: the onset of mental
incompetency in a loved one.

When the onset of incompetency is gradual, we may respond as Fiona
did, with a feeling of panic, of wondering what can be happening, thinking that this must just be a "bad day" and that all will soon be back to normal. We want to see the person as we always have—capable, independent,
and in control.

In other cases, mental incompetency happens in a tragic instant with
a sudden occurrence such as an accident or a stroke leaving brain damage
in its wake. Whether such damage is serious or minor, the person's ability
to make independent decisions is diminished overnight, and loved ones
are left to figure out how to proceed.

Gaining Some control

A couple of thoughts may be helpful to a family trying to cope during a
difficult and uncertain time. First, it's important to keep in mind that often
the individual experiencing failing mental health or suffering brain damage

is still, to some extent at least, the same person that he or she has always been … the person simply needs some assistance with making decisions that previously would have been made independently. The key is to try to ascertain where the line is between important and helpful intervention, on the one hand, and allowing the person as much autonomy and independence as is possible, on the other.

Two Types of Decisions

When it comes to assisting an incompetent person with decision-making, there are two main areas of concern: those decisions that address financial matters of all types—assets, liabilities, income sources, and expenses; and those decisions that have to do with personal care or health care, such as whether to proceed with a particular medical treatment.

Financial Decisions

Decision-making of a financial nature includes the investment, saving, and spending of money assets, but also the protection of all other assets owned by a person, such as land, a house, artwork, and so on. Many of these types of assets will require insurance decisions to be made, and opportunities to sell the assets will arise. There may also be sources of income that need to be looked after, expenses to pay, and in some cases, for example, if incompetency happened overnight because of an accident, even businesses to be managed. These types of decisions can be delegated to someone else (called the "attorney," but that doesn't mean the person needs to be a lawyer!) in a document called a power of attorney.

Personal Care Decisions

Personal care decisions run the gamut from personal hygiene (how often to bathe and have manicures) to serious medical decisions such as the consent to emergency surgery and the continuation of life support systems. Personal care decisions typically also involve where an individual should live and the types of activities in which he or she will participate. To delegate these types of decisions to someone else—after incompetency has occurred—a document called a "living will," "power of attorney for personal care," or "personal directive" (the term may vary depending on the jurisdiction) is used.

Advance Planning ... or Not?

With these two types of decision-making in mind, the next step for the family or close friends to investigate is whether the individual did any advance planning. This can be very helpful, as Fiona discovered!

Often such planning is done in conjunction with a will, so it may be useful to begin by checking with the individual's lawyer about the possible existence of a power of attorney (for financial decisions) and a personal directive (for personal care decisions).

(Don't worry about the particular fancy names by which these two types of documents are called where you live. Either the lawyer holding the documents will be able to sort them out for you, or reading the documents carefully will reveal to you whether they cover financial or personal care decision-making.)

If the individual's lawyer didn't prepare such documents, don't give up yet. The person you are concerned about may have stored these documents in a safety deposit box, a filing cabinet at home, or perhaps with a good friend.

If you locate documents looking like a power of attorney and/or a "living will" or personal directive, review the documents to determine how and when they may be used.

Using a Power of Attorney

An old-fashioned type of power of attorney is valid only as long as the person who signed it is still mentally competent. (Sometimes a power of attorney signed at a retail bank branch is this type of document.) Unfortunately, a power of attorney that is invalid once mental incompetency occurs is obviously not much use if the person has already lost his or her competency!

Ideally you will have located a power of attorney that is "enduring" or "durable" in nature, which simply means that it survives past the person's competency—exactly the situation you are now in!

An enduring type of power of attorney may be written so that it can be used as soon as it is signed—or it may be written so that it can only be used once the person who signed it becomes incompetent.

If the document is the type that becomes effective only when incompetency occurs, you will need to determine how incompetency is defined in the power of attorney. Many enduring powers of attorney—such as the one signed by Fiona's dad—state that incompetency will be deemed to have occurred if and when two medical doctors state in writing that the individual can no longer make reasonable decisions for him- or herself. Other powers of attorney may require only one doctor or a trusted friend or relative to make the certification.

If the applicable triggering event or contingency is clear simply by reading the document, all you need to do is obtain the necessary paperwork. For example, if the certification of two medical doctors is needed, you would arrange for the person to be examined by two doctors so that those medical certificates could be obtained and attached to the power of attorney.

On the other hand, if the document is at all unclear, you would be wise to visit or call a lawyer who regularly prepares such documents to obtain a professional opinion on the next steps. If possible, call the lawyer who prepared the actual document you are looking at—there may in fact be medical forms available from that lawyer that can simply be completed by the required number of doctors and attached to the power of attorney.

A lawyer will also be able to review the entire document and advise the named attorney as to his or her exact duties and powers. The power of attorney may contain restrictions, such as forbidding the attorney from selling certain real estate. On the other hand, the power of attorney may also contain some specific powers, such as the power to use some of the incompetent person's assets to help grandchildren with university tuition. Without a specific power like this in the document, the attorney is required by law to use the assets only for the benefit of the incompetent person.

Using a Living Will or Personal Directive

The other type of decision-making that needs to be addressed when a person has lost or is losing competency are those decisions relating to personal care and health care. Advance planning, if it has been done, will be in the form of a document called something like a living will or personal directive. Again, don't worry about the name of the document.

For many years now in Canada, the law has been evolving on how and when people can stipulate in advance their wishes on health and personal care matters. Accordingly, it is accurate to say that there are many, many different types of documents out there, some of which will be legally valid and binding, and others which, frankly, will not be binding. It is therefore really important to have any such document reviewed by a lawyer familiar with such matters, so that you can determine exactly what authority, if any, the incompetent person has been able to convey by way of the document.

In the worst case, the document is merely a confusing or ambiguous statement of wishes—such as a request to not have "heroic measures" engaged in to prolong life. In such cases, the wording often does not even reflect the person's real thoughts and ideas, but was simply a form document that seemed like a "good idea at the time"! This type of so-called living will may very well not be binding on the medical profession, if, in fact, it is even worded in such a manner that makes sense and provides clear direction to the responsible health care practitioners.

In the best case scenario, the now-incompetent person will have signed a document in accordance with his or her provincial legislation. Done properly, such a document will clearly set out some binding decisions about personal and health care matters and will often also appoint a trusted person to act as the decision-maker on any matters not covered off specifically. This type of appointment enables the named "agent," so to speak, to step right in and make the personal and health care decisions that, to the best of the agent's knowledge and belief, the incompetent person would have made if he or she was still capable of doing so.

If no Advance Planning has been Done ... Then What?

Many Canadians do not even have a will in place, so you can be sure that even more have not done the advance planning required to address the possibility of incompetency! It's not surprising, then, that even the most thorough search for such advance planning documents may turn up nothing.

All is not lost! The law in each Canadian province allows a court application to be made that—if all the evidence is in place about incompetency—results in a court order appointing a substitute decision-maker for the incompetent person. Usually the name used for the financial decision-maker is "trustee" and the name for the personal or health care decision-maker is "guardian." If you are putting yourself forward as the proposed guardian or trustee, you can always represent yourself in a court of law, after having figured out the court documents that need to be filed and so on. However, it is unusual for a person to do the legal work. It is well worth your time to search out a lawyer who specializes in this field, and get his or her help. Not only will the lawyer be able to do the court application expeditiously, he or she will advise you on your ongoing duties and responsibilities as a substitute decision-maker.

This advice about being a trustee and/or a guardian is very important because, as a trustee, you will be acting as fiduciary—caring for another person's property. And, as a guardian, you will be called upon to make some very serious personal decisions. To avoid conflict, these responsibilities of the trustee and guardian include communication with other people (family members and close friends) who also care about the well-being of the incompetent person.

Accordingly, rest assured that the courts are extremely strict about how these jobs are carried out. It will be necessary to account to the court on a regular basis for the work you do and the decisions you make as an incompetent person's trustee or guardian, so you will want to be clear from the outset how these important tasks should be carried out. One of the most important topics the lawyer will discuss with you is the fact that you cannot benefit yourself or anyone else (other than the incompetent person) by your decisions. Unfortunately, there are trustees each year who, due to ignorance or to dishonesty, use some of the other person's property or income for their own benefit, or for the benefit of someone else. For example, a trustee may think that since Grandma is 95, and her children have big mortgages, it makes sense to pay these mortgages from Grandma's large investment account. *No!* This would be a fundamental breach of trust, and a trustee who does this will be required to account to the court, and at a minimum, make full restitution to the dependent adult.

In Short

In summary, the law looks at each person as having two components: the financial side and the personal side. If incompetency occurs, or seems to be occurring, in a loved one, the best bet is to find out immediately if the person has done some advance planning to address the need for a substitute decision-maker. As you work through what needs to be done, it will help to keep in the front of your mind these two categories—financial and personal—and the two possible scenarios—advance planning done versus no planning done. Good luck!

THE *Menu*

⊷⊷⊶

Fresh oysters with mango pickle salsa

Saffron wild rice pilaf with chorizo, prawns,
sweet peppers, and corn

Romaine salad with coriander aïoli and roasted pepitas

Homemade focaccia

Orange mascarpone trifle with toasted hazelnut sponge cake

⊷⊷⊶

Fresh oysters with mango pickle salsa   SERVES 8

Mango pickle*

2	ripe, but firm, mangoes, peeled and cut into ¼-inch (5mm) slices	2
½ cup	sugar	125 ml
½-inch piece	fresh ginger, thinly sliced	1 cm piece
2 cloves	garlic, sliced in quarters, lengthwise	2 cloves
½ tsp.	whole black peppercorns, coarsely cracked	2 ml
½ tsp.	finely chopped fresh chilies	2 mL
1 tsp.	salt	5 mL
½ cup	white vinegar	125 mL

1. Pack the mango slices into a glass jar.

2. In a small saucepan, combine the sugar, ginger, garlic, peppercorns, chilies, and salt. Cook over medium heat until warm and fragrant, approximately 1 minute.

3. Remove the pan from the heat. Add the vinegar and stir until the sugar has completely dissolved.

4. Pour the vinegar mixture slowly into the jar over the mango slices. Refrigerate overnight before using or for up to 2 weeks.

---

*Adapted from Marcia Kiesel, "Mangoes," *Food and Wine*, June 1995, 57.

Mango pickle salsa*

1 jar	mango pickle,	1 jar
	cut into ¼-inch (5mm) dice	
¼	red onion, cut into ⅛-inch (3mm) dice	¼
1 tbsp.	chopped fresh coriander	15 mL
½-tsp.	finely chopped fresh chilies (optional)	2 ml
	Salt and pepper, to taste	

Combine all ingredients. Refrigerate for up to 4 days.

For 24 to 30 oysters*

1. Using a firm brush, clean the oysters under cold, running water.

2. Immediately before serving, shuck the oysters as follows: Hold the oyster, flat side down on a firm, solid surface, using a clean tea towel to protect your hand. Slide an oyster blade or dinner knife (not one from your best set and *never* a sharp knife) between the top and bottom shells and gently twist the shells apart. Loosen the oyster, taking care to not spill the liquid inside.

3. Place the oysters on a bed of crushed ice, rock salt, or simply a chilled plate. Spoon a small amount of the salsa onto each oyster.

* Use the freshest oysters available, regardless of the breed. Buy from a reputable fish dealer—someone you trust, as opposed to a supermarket, where proper storage may not be available.

---

*Adapted from Marcia Kiesel, "Mangoes," *Food and Wine*, June 1995, 57.

Saffron wild rice pilaf with chorizo, prawns, SERVES 8
sweet peppers, and corn

*This one-dish meal is ideally suited to serving a crowd. It will serve eight, gener-
ously, and is light, but satisfying. Fresh scallops or clams may be added or used in
place of the prawns, as long as the cardinal rule of shellfish is observed—don't
overcook.*

1 cup	dry white wine	250 ml
½ cup	wild rice	125 mL
½ tsp.	salt	2 mL
½ lb.	chorizo or other spicy, fresh (as opposed to smoked) sausage	250 g
4 tsp.	olive oil	20 mL
1	onion, chopped	1
1	large red bell pepper or a mix of red and yellow bell peppers, cut into small dice	1
2 tsp.	ground cumin	10 mL
1 cup	long grain white rice	250 mL
1 clove	garlic, minced	1 clove
1 large can (26 ounce)	tomatoes, finely chopped, with liquid	(796 mL)
½ tsp.	saffron threads, lightly packed	2 mL
1 tbsp.	butter	15 mL
½ lb.	fresh prawns, peeled and deveined	250 g
1 cup	frozen sweet corn, thawed	250 mL
1½ cups	cooked black beans, or 1 – 14 oz. (398 mL) can, rinsed and drained	375 ml
	Grated zest of 1 lemon	
1 tbsp.	finely chopped chervil or parsley	15 ml

1. In a medium saucepan, bring 2½ cups (625 mL) water and ½ cup (125 mL) white wine to a boil. Add the wild rice, and ½ tsp. (2 mL) of salt. Bring the mixture back to a boil, then reduce heat and simmer, covered. When the rice is tender (after approximately 1 hour), drain and set aside, covered, to retain heat.

2. Put the sausage and 1 cup (250 mL) water in a large, ovenproof sauté pan. Partially cover it with a lid and bring it to a boil. Turn down the heat and simmer until the water has evaporated, approximately 10 minutes. Remove the cover. Brown the sausage, turning it occasionally, about another 5 minutes, until cooked through. If the pan begins to burn, quickly deglaze it with a small amount of water. Remove the sausage from the pan and set it aside. Do not wash the pan. When the sausage is cool enough to handle, cut it into ¼-inch (5 mm) thick slices.

3. Heat the oven to 350ºF (180°C). Heat the olive oil in the sausage pan over medium-high heat. Add the onion, bell pepper, and cumin. Cook until the vegetables are steamy and a bit soft. Add the white rice and garlic and cook another 3 to 5 minutes, until the rice has absorbed some of the oil. Add the tomatoes and their juice, the remaining ½ cup (125 mL) wine, 1 cup (250 mL) water, and saffron. Bring to a boil, scraping the caramelized bits from the bottom of the pan. Remove from the heat, cover tightly with foil, and place in the oven. Bake for approximately 25 minutes, or until the rice is tender.

4. In a small sauté pan, heat the butter over medium-high heat until it begins to brown. Add the prawns. Sauté them until they are pink and barely translucent, just a few minutes. Remove them from the hot pan, as you don't want them to continue cooking, and set aside. Again, don't wash the pan just yet.

5. While the shrimp pan and burner are still hot, add the sliced sausage and sauté until heated through and brown. Deglaze the pan with ¼ cup (50 mL) water, then add the corn and beans. Simmer for approximately 2 minutes.

6. Add the wild rice, prawns, and sausage mixture to the white rice, and gently stir in the lemon zest and chervil.

Romaine salad with coriander aïoli and roasted pepitas   SERVES 8

Coriander chutney, a marvellous product available at Middle Eastern stores, as well as some supermarkets, is made from, among other things, garlic and fresh coriander, often called cilantro. This is a very easy, and immensely popular salad, probably due to the fact that the flavours, though complex, aren't overly challenging. Great for a crowd—even kids like it!

1 cup	dry white wine	250 ml
½ cup	mayonnaise*	125 ml
1 tbsp.	coriander chutney	15 mL
1 tsp.	fresh lime juice	5 mL
	Pinch of white pepper	
1	large head romaine lettuce, trimmed of outer leaves, washed, dried, and cut into bite sized pieces	1
3 tbsp.	roasted, salted pepitas (pumpkin seeds)	50 mL

* Don't use low-fat mayonnaise. If you must, replace one-third of the mayonnaise with plain yogurt, or make a different salad.

1. In a small bowl, whisk together the mayonnaise, coriander chutney, lime juice, and white pepper. If necessary, add salt to taste.

2. In a large bowl, combine the lettuce and half the dressing, and gently mix. Very clean hands are the perfect tool for this job, with a rubber spatula placing a distant second. Add more dressing as needed, being very careful not to overdress the greens.

3. Transfer the greens to a serving bowl and sprinkle them evenly with the pepitas. Serve at once.

Homemade focaccia*   SERVES 8

This is a basic flatbread recipe that can be easily modified to suit any taste. Mix your favourite herbs into the dough; replace half the water with homemade tomato sauce or puréed roasted red peppers; or top with thinly sliced tomatoes and red onions and sprinkle with grated fresh Parmesan cheese, fresh basil, salt, and freshly ground black pepper.

½ tsp.	sugar	2 mL
1½ cups	warm water	375 mL
1½ tsp.	dry yeast	7 mL
3 cups, approx.	white bread flour	750 mL, approx.
¼ cup	olive oil, plus 2 tbsp.	50 mL, plus 25 mL
1 tbsp.	salt	15 mL

1. In the bowl of an electric mixer, dissolve the sugar in the warm water. Add the yeast and allow it to sit until the surface is bubbly and the yeast has dissolved. Add 1 cup (250 mL) of flour, the olive oil, and

salt. Mix, using a dough hook, until the dough on the hook and the dough in the bowl are still attached by long and very elastic strands when you raise the hook from the bowl. Lower the hook and cover the bowl with plastic wrap. Allow the dough to sit until it has doubled in volume, approximately one hour.

2. Resume mixing the dough, and add flour ½ cup (125 mL) at a time until a soft, slightly sticky dough forms.

3. Sprinkle some flour on a clean work surface, and turn out the dough. Knead it by hand, adding more flour as needed until a soft, smooth dough forms. (You may not need all the flour).

4. Brush a large bowl with 1 tablespoon (15 mL) of olive oil. Shape the dough into a ball, put it into a bowl, and brush the surface with oil. Cover the bowl with plastic wrap. Place it in a warm, not hot, spot for approximately 1½ hours, until doubled in bulk, or in the refrigerator, overnight.

5. Brush the back of a large sheet pan with the remaining 1 tablespoon (15 mL) of olive oil. Turn the dough out onto the sheet and with oiled hands, flatten out the dough to about ½ inch (1 cm) thick. Using your finger tips or your knuckles, dimple the dough, taking care not to poke through it. Cover and allow to rise until doubled in bulk, about 1½ hours, or longer if it has been refrigerated.

6. Heat oven to 400ºF (200°C). Bake the focaccia on the centre rack of the oven for about 20 minutes, until it is golden and firm enough to handle. Working quickly, remove the baking sheet from the oven, loosen the bread with a thin, metal spatula, and slide the bread off the sheet directly onto the centre rack of the oven. Bake another 5 minutes, or until evenly browned and hollow sounding when tapped.

7. Cool on a rack and, as tempting as it may be, don't cut it while it's still hot.

* If you do not own a stand mixer, you can easily make the focaccia by hand. Simply follow steps 1 and 2 using a large bowl and a wooden spoon, preferably bamboo, for its strength.

Orange mascarpone trifle with toasted hazelnut sponge cake

SERVES 12+

Assemble the trifle a day before serving to allow all the flavours to blend.

Toasted Hazelnut Sponge Cake

Once you've made this cake, you'll want to add it to your regular repertoire of quick and easy desserts. Try cutting it into four even pieces and layered with jam or fresh fruit, and whipped cream; spread it with lemon curd and roll it like a jelly roll; or spread chocolate mousse between two layers of cake and create dessert "sandwiches."

¾ cup	all-purpose flour	175 mL
½ cup	ground, toasted hazelnuts*	125 mL
¼ tsp.	baking powder	1 mL
5	eggs, at room temperature	5
	Pinch of salt	
½ tsp.	Frangelico (hazelnut liqueur)	2 mL
½ cup	sugar	125 mL

* Spread 2 to 3 ounces of sliced hazelnuts on a baking sheet. Toast the hazelnuts for 5-7 minutes in a 300ºF (150ºC) oven, until lightly browned. Using a food processor, process the nuts to a fine crumb.

1. Heat the oven to 375ºF (190°C). Line an 11 x 17-inch (27 x 42 cm) baking sheet with parchment paper.

2. In a small bowl, combine the flour, hazelnuts, and baking powder. Mix until well blended. Set aside.

3. In a large bowl, beat the eggs, salt, and Frangelico on medium-high speed until foamy. Gradually add the sugar and beat for 10 to 15 minutes, until the mixture is very pale, light, and has quadrupled in volume. (When the whisk is lifted, the mixture will fall back into the bowl, forming a ribbon that lingers a bit on the surface.)

4. Gently fold one-third of the dry ingredients into the whipped eggs until they are partially incorporated. Repeat twice. Do not overmix.

5. Pour the batter evenly into the prepared baking sheet and bake for 6-8 minutes, until the cake is golden brown and slightly springy when touched.

6. Remove the cake, along with the parchment paper, from the baking sheet and cool on a wire rack. Invert the cake onto a cutting board and peel away the parchment paper. Cut the cake into strips approximately 1 x 5 inches (2.5 x 11 cm).

Orange mascarpone pastry cream

2 cups plus ½ cup	milk (not low-fat)	500 mL, plus 125 mL
½ cup	sugar	125 mL
¼ cup	corn starch	50 mL
	Grated zest from 1 orange	
1	egg	1
2	egg yolks	2
1 tbsp.	butter, softened	15 mL
½ tsp.	vanilla extract	2 mL
1 cup	mascarpone cheese, softened	250 mL
1 cup	heavy cream (35 % M.F.), whipped to soft peaks	250 mL

1. In a medium saucepan, scald 2 cups (500 mL) of milk.

2. In a bowl, whisk together the ½ cup (125 mL) milk, sugar, corn starch, orange zest, egg, and yolks.

3. Stir in about one-third of the hot milk to the egg mixture. Mix well, and pour the whole mixture back into the remaining hot milk.

4. Cook the custard, stirring constantly with a rubber spatula, until it begins to boil. Immediately turn the heat down to low, and cook until the custard is the consistency of stirred yogurt. Strain it through a sieve into a glass or stainless steel bowl. Stir in the butter and vanilla. Cover the surface directly with plastic wrap and cool to room temperature.

5. Beat the softened mascarpone into the custard until smooth, with no visible lumps. Refrigerate 2 to 3 hours. Whip the cream until soft peaks form.

6. Vigorously mix the custard to ensure that the temperature and consistency are uniform throughout. Spoon one-third of the whipped cream into the custard and stir gently to mix. Fold in the remaining whipped cream, cover, and refrigerate.

Assembly

1 ½ cups	heavy cream (35% M.F.)	375 mL
1 tbsp.	sugar	15 mL
¼ cup plus 1 tsp.	Grand Marnier	50 mL, plus 5 mL
1	recipe toasted hazelnut sponge cake*	1
1	recipe orange mascarpone pastry cream	1
⅔ cup	finely chopped or grated white chocolate	150 mL
2 ½ pounds	fresh navel oranges, segmented, and free of membrane and pith	1.25 kg
2 tbsp.	finely chopped, toasted hazelnuts	25 mL

* Or pound cake from your favourite bakery (cut into fingers).

1. Whip together the cream, sugar, and 1 teaspoon (5 mL) of Grand Marnier until a medium-firm peak is formed when you lift the whisk.

2. In a glass or crystal bowl, arrange a loose layer of sponge cake. Brush the sponge cake with Grand Marnier.

3. Spread one-third of the orange segments evenly over the cake, making sure that some of the segments are touching the sides of the bowl.

4. Spread one-third of the pastry cream over the oranges.

5. Scatter one-third of the grated white chocolate evenly over the pastry cream.

6. Spread one-third of the whipped cream over the chocolate.

7. Repeat twice more, sprinkling the final layer of whipped cream with chopped hazelnuts.

Advance Preparation

Two days before the dinner:

1. Pickle the mangoes.

2. Make the hazelnut sponge cake.

3. Prepare the mascarpone pastry cream through step 5.

The day before the dinner:

1. Finish the mascarpone pastry cream and assemble the trifle.

2. Prepare the focaccia dough and refrigerate.

The day of the dinner:

<u>A.M.</u>

1. Finish the focaccia.

2. Prepare the coriander aïoli.

3. Peel and clean the prawns.

4. Make the mango pickle salsa.

5. Wash and cut romaine lettuce. Wrap in paper towels, place in a plastic bag, and refrigerate.

P.M.

1. Cut and measure all ingredients for the saffron rice and set aside. Refrigerate all perishables.

2. Clean oysters.

Shortly before the guests arrive

1. Cut focaccia into squares or triangles. Put them in a bowl or basket covered with plastic wrap.

2. Cook wild rice. It will take about an hour, so plan accordingly. You may also cook the sausage at this time.

3. Shuck some but not all of the oysters and dress with salsa. Put them on a plate and refrigerate.

When your guests begin to arrive, put out a few of the oysters at a time.

January

FUSION Comfort FOOD

Todd was always filled with a pleasant feeling of anticipation when a shipment arrived at Nori's Home and Botanical. Since Todd (and Nori, whenever she could get away) made a point of personally searching out new items for the store, the arrival of a packing crate usually triggered happy memories of time spent under a hot foreign sun. When Todd inspected the packing slip and saw that the shipment was Majolica ware from Umbria, he began to laugh.

"What's so funny?" asked Nori as she brushed by him with two floral arrangements ready to be stowed in the delivery truck.

"I was just remembering the day we ordered this stuff. There we were, setting off from Perugia for a nice little day trip. Who would have guessed we'd have a cloudburst and have to deal with getting the top up on the Fiat? I'll never forget the sight of you trying to translate the manual with the rain pouring down!"

"Oh yeah," said Nori with a laugh. "Well, at least I figured it out in the end, which is more than I can say for you when the windshield wiper fell off on the way back. That's the last time we rent a convertible in the rainy season!"

After prying the cover off the packing crate, Todd reached into the depths of shredded newspaper and straw and was immediately rewarded with a beautiful cerulean blue platter with a simple design of intertwined grape leaves.

"Wow!" said Nori. "They're even more beautiful than I remembered. Let me get in there, too."

Within minutes, drifts of packing material covered the floor and a pile of platters and bowls stood on the shelves, their luscious colours gleaming under a glaze as slick as rain from an Umbrian sky.

"Don't we have the best business in the world?" said Nori, kissing Todd and picking an errant piece of straw from his hair.

Todd's answer was interrupted by a buzz from the intercom—"Can you take Line 1, please, Todd? It sounds kind of urgent."

"I guess I'd better take that, Nori … but yes, you're right, we do."

⁂

When Todd came to find her a few minutes later, Nori immediately knew something was wrong.

"What is it, Todd? You look like you've seen a ghost!"

"That was Denise Arsenault … she said that Scott's been killed."

"Killed! You've got to be kidding—no, of course you're not, but how? How could it have happened? Didn't you have a beer with him just last week?"

"Apparently, he was driving back from B.C. with Theresa—you know, she was the first real girlfriend he'd had since the divorce from Denise. They were on that stretch of the Trans-Canada near Golden—there was a sudden snow squall and they were ploughed into by a semi travelling on the wrong side of the road. Denise said that Scott died instantly and Theresa died in hospital a few hours later."

"Oh, Todd, I'm so sorry. You two were really close, weren't you?" said Nori with a look of concern. She rubbed Todd's shoulder gently. "How many years do you go back?"

"I met Scott in Grade One. Mrs. Vaughan asked us to share the job of looking after the hamster. I couldn't stand cleaning out the cage—all those soggy bits of lettuce and smelly pellets. Scott was still ragging me about it when I was best man at his wedding, 20 years later."

"Poor Scott," said Nori. "What a horrible way to die, and his girl-friend, too! Had they been going out long?"

"About six months, I think. The last time I played squash with Scott he told me he was crazy about her. I'm sure if this … this accident … hadn't happened, they'd have been married by the end of the year. Scott was really heartbroken when things didn't work out with Denise. Some guys are just meant to be married…."

"And other guys aren't," finished Nori. She kissed Todd on the cheek. "At least he and Theresa didn't have any children. I guess that's one good thing in this whole mess."

"That's true," said Todd, "but, of course, he did have the two boys with Denise. She broke down on the phone just now, wondering how she's going to tell them. Scott thought the world of those little guys and he really looked forward to his weekends and holidays with them. I know for a fact that he paid more for their support than they had agreed to. Denise really appreciated that. She'd cut back to working part-time so she could be there for the boys."

"Is there any way you can help?" asked Nori.

"I said I'd go over tonight and take the boys to indoor soccer. They both have a practice at 6:30. Denise will tell them when we get back. Damn."

"Oh, Todd, that's going to be so tough for her. Is there anything *I* can do to help?" "Well, I could tell you that I don't have time to clean up all this mess," said Todd gesturing at the straw-strewn floor, "but that wouldn't exactly be the truth. I'll give it a quick sweep and leave the rest of the unpacking until tomorrow—there's nothing that can't keep. Don't worry about keeping dinner for me —I'll have a quick burger with Brent and Danny. I'll probably be back around 9."

⤜᷈᷈⤛

The next morning Nori awoke abruptly at 5:30, sensing Todd was not in bed beside her. She immediately remembered the news of Scott's death and felt her stomach twisting into a tight knot. In her three years with Todd, Nori had come to realize the importance of the two men's friendship. Through childhood crises, teenage angst, loss of jobs, and failed marriages, they had been there for each other without reservation.

Nori reached for her robe and slipped down to the kitchen. As she waited for the espresso machine light to come on, the front door opened, letting in a blast of freezing cold air.

"Todd? I wondered where you were. Don't tell me you were out jogging—it's got to be 30 below!"

"I really needed to clear my head—I don't think I slept very well."

"Tell me about it. I thought I was sharing a bed with a pro wrestler!"

"Sorry, Nori. Hey, come here and warm me up. My face is numb with the cold."

"That's the best offer I've had this morning. We could always go back to bed, you know."

"Don't I wish," said Todd, "but the truth is I've got a ton of stuff to do today. I want to clear the decks as much as I can. Something tells me Denise may need some help with making arrangements over the next little while."

"Gee, I hadn't even thought about the funeral," said Nori. "Will there be a service here or what?"

"Scott's family's located all over the map but Denise has spoken with his mom and I think the body's going to be cremated here and the ashes sent to her in Winnipeg."

Todd paused and looked away, embarrassed by the tears welling up in his eyes. "I still can't believe it. Here I am talking about ashes and last week I was having a beer with the guy."

෴

Todd was relieved that the rest of the day flew by—it was good to have his mind occupied by other matters. There were the remaining crates of Majolica to be unpacked, washed, entered into inventory, and priced, a lengthy meeting with their accountant to be endured, and even a stint delivering flowers for Nori when their regular driver had to take himself off to the dentist with an abscessed tooth. By the afternoon, a chinook had blown in with a heady rush of warm air and the roads were rivers of melting ice.

"Want to stop off for a bite at Federico's tonight?" asked Nori.

"Sure, that sounds great. I don't feel much like cooking tonight, anyway, and I think it's my turn."

"I *know* it's your turn," said Nori with a laugh. "Let's just eat out."

෴

Back at home after a good meal and some relaxing conversation, Todd put the kettle on for tea while Nori went to check their messages.

"Denise called. She wants you to call back as soon as possible."

"Oh, great," Todd groaned. "I hope the boys aren't having too rough a time. I guess I should call her from the den. Can you get the kettle when it boils?"

Five minutes later, Todd walked back into the kitchen and for the second time in two days Nori asked him if he had seen a ghost.

"That bad, eh? No, I guess I'm sort of in shock, though. Denise called her lawyer this afternoon. I guess it occurred to her that if Todd's bank account was frozen, this might prevent Todd's support payments coming through as usual."

"That sounds a bit mercenary, doesn't it?" asked Nori.

"Well, like I told you, she and the boys really depend on those payments. I don't blame her for being concerned. Anyway, her lawyer calls Scott's lawyer and guess what *he* says?"

"I haven't got a clue."

"He tells her that some guy named Todd Reimer is the executor of Scott's estate."

"*You?* But, Todd, he couldn't just have done that without asking you, could he?"

"No, that's the bizarre part. At first I couldn't remember that we'd ever discussed it and then it came back to me. It was about a year ago when I was helping him move some furniture into his new place. He was telling me how his lawyer said he needed to redo his will after he and Denise split up. And then I *think* he asked me to be his executor. Jeez, at the time I was probably holding up the end of a sofa. I didn't give it another thought. Well, why would I? When a 38-year-old guy is talking about his estate, that sounds so far off in the future...."

"Except if he dies a year later," said Nori, finishing his thought. "What does being an executor entail exactly?"

"God, how should I know? I guess I said yes the same way I said yes when he asked me to be his best man. You know me—plunge right in and ask the questions later. Now I'm in way over my head."

"Well, there must be someone who can help you. This must happen all the time—what do other people do?"

"Denise has given me the name and number of Scott's lawyer. I guess he's my man, just as soon as I can get an appointment. What an idiot I've been—I can hardly figure out our GST payments! Why would anyone trust me to take care of their affairs?"

"Oh, come on, Todd! You're way smarter at that financial stuff than you like to make out. Besides, that's why God invented accountants and lawyers. I'm sure they'll tell you what needs to be done and maybe you'll just have to make some decisions. Don't get too worked up about it yet."

"Time will tell, I guess, but maybe we should call our old buddy John and see if he can spare some time to help you out in the store. Something tells me I'm going to have my hands full for the next little while."

⊷∞⊷

The chinook conditions were a distant memory a few weeks later when it was Todd and Nori's turn to host the dinner club meeting.

"Hi Vanessa! Hi Gerald! Come on in—Fiona and the Enrights are already here. In fact, I've already set Doug to work throwing more logs on the fire."

Vanessa and Gerald walked through to the kitchen, Vanessa carrying a large melon, Gerald balancing a pile of plastic containers filled with the rest of the salad ingredients.

"Sometimes I think we should do one of those progressive things," muttered Gerald. "You know, eat one course at one place and then move on to the next. It would save all this moving around of food."

"Yes, but then we'd *all* have to clean our houses," said Sheila, "instead of just the hosts having to do it!"

"Sheila's right, Gerald. Besides, don't be such an old grouch," said Vanessa. "I love coming over to Todd and Nori's, everything is always so interesting. Just look at these beautiful flowers—I was wondering what

you might have in store for us, Nori. They seem to be perfectly in keeping with our Japanese theme tonight."

Nori explained, "When I was growing up, my grandmother was
always at me to take lessons in *ikebana*—the art of Japanese flower
arrangement. Of course, like any typical teenager, I resisted on principle.
Then, when I was in my 20s, being Japanese suddenly became trendy so
I decided to sign up for some classes. I never suspected at the time that it
would lead to a career as a florist."

"I suppose there must be quite a bit of philosophy behind these traditional arrangements," said Fiona.

"Oh, there's an enormous amount of philosophy. With my one year
of study, I only scratched the surface—some people dedicate their entire
lives to it."

"Really!" exclaimed Fiona. "How extraordinary—no disrespect, Nori,
but there must be just so many ways you can stick some flowers in a pot.
What's the thinking behind that arrangement on the dining room table,
for instance?"

"That's a *jikuya*, or freestyle arrangement. It's much more open to cre-
ativity than any of the other styles. In *jikuya*, a piece is created to express
the artist's idea or emotions."

"So can anyone guess what Nori was feeling when she put this piece
together?" asked Sheila. "I think you might have to give us a clue, Nori."

"Actually, in the last little while I've been thinking a lot about the
unpredictability of life, and death for that matter," Nori replied.

"Wow, heav-y!" said Doug. "What brought that on?"

"It seems that Todd has been named the executor of an estate—his
best friend died just a few weeks ago. It's been sort of a nightmare. I expect
Todd will tell you about it over dinner. In the meantime, I guess we
should get this show on the road."

Todd came in from the kitchen and invited everyone to be seated at the dining table. "Nori and I have had quite a discussion over seating arrangements. To get the full Japanese dining experience, I thought she'd want us to sit on the floor."

"I'd never inflict that on anyone over the age of 30—it's just too damned uncomfortable! Besides, tonight's menu is Fusion—not traditional Japanese food," said Nori, carrying in two pale green soup plates that perfectly complemented their sunny orange contents—Fiona's yam and ginger bisque.

"Thank God!" said Gerald. "I mean thank God that we get to sit in chairs, not thank God we don't have to eat traditional Japanese food!"

Todd filled everyone's sake cups from a warmed ceramic beaker, and Doug proposed a toast to the New Year. "May we all enjoy good health, good friends, and happiness!"

"Haven't done too well on that front, so far," said Todd.

"No, Nori said something about you losing your friend recently," Sheila said with a look of concern. "What happened?"

"Well, the terrible tragedy is that my buddy was killed a few weeks ago—same age as me—but on top of all the shock and stuff, I found out I'm the executor of his estate! He'd asked me, of course, and I guess I'd said yes and then put it right out of my mind. And the ironic thing is that Nori and I still haven't got our own wills in place and here I am—an executor, for God's sake!"

"Good heavens!" said Vanessa. "I'm sure you must be reeling. Did your friend have a family?"

"Yes," replied Todd. "He was divorced from his wife but he was the proud dad of two terrific little boys. A 'non-custodial parent,' I think they call it—I'm beginning to have to get my head around all these legal terms."

"Let me help you clear these soup plates, Todd," said Doug. "I don't want to miss this. My mother has named *me* as her executor. I'm the same as you—I just said yes without even thinking what I'm in for."

"I hardly have a clue yet myself—I guess I'll have a much better idea over the next few months. We could get together for lunch some time and I could fill you in—that's if I still have a life. Sometimes I imagine I'm going to be like one of those characters in a Dickens novel, scratching away in a ledger with a great heap of legal documents ready to bury me at any moment."

In the kitchen, Vanessa was putting the finishing touches to her dish. "I'm glad you gave me this recipe to make, Nori. I've prepared ceviche before, but only the Latin American version—this is much more Asian in flavour with the cilantro and the peanuts. I gave some to Gerald to try— he's not a big sushi fan but he sure liked this!"

"That's good," said Nori. "The citric acid in the lime juice really cooks the halibut so it doesn't have that raw fish taste that some people don't care for."

After Vanessa had arranged the ceviche in black lacquered bowls, the two women took the next course into the dining room.

☙❦❧

Nori looked around the table with interest. "I'm impressed. I put out regular cutlery, just in case, but I see that everyone has used chopsticks. We haven't even had that much sake yet!"

"I think I have," said Fiona, her cheeks somewhat flushed. "I wasn't sure I would like it but it tastes so warm and nice."

"The sake's good but that ceviche was really great," said Sheila. "Way better than the oyster you got me to choke back last time. I think I might even make this recipe some time—what do you think, Doug? It's kind of fun to try something new, isn't it?"

"Yep, I'm always up to try something new—like being an executor, for example. You will keep me posted, Todd, won't you?"

"Oh, sure. I'm just beginning to think I'm in the wrong business— I should have gone to law school. I tell you, what I *don't* know just amazes me."

"Like what?" asked Doug with interest.

"This has got nothing to do with being an executor but I was checking on a few things with *my* lawyer. I mentioned how this whole business with Scott had given me the impetus to get my own affairs sorted out. She said I should come in and bring my wife. When I said that Nori was my partner and not my wife, she said even more reason for her to come in."

"What do you mean—your business partner?" asked Fiona.

"Well, she is that, too," said Todd, "but, no, I meant that we aren't legally married."

"Does that complicate matters from the standpoint of the business?" Fiona wondered.

"No, that's all taken care of. We've had a partnership agreement for the business since day one. No, the problem comes if I should suddenly die, like Scott. Luckily, he had a will in place but if I died without having gotten around to doing up a will, who knows what would happen?"

"There are laws, aren't there, that govern these things?" asked Doug.

"That's what I thought," said Todd with a rueful smile. "But apparently it's not that easy. Some provinces have laws that treat a so-called co-habitant as a spouse, other provinces don't. It's very confusing! I think everyone, including the politicians, has a different idea of what a common-law relationship is."

"We certainly proved that," said Nori. "When Todd came home from the lawyer he asked me what I thought was the rule governing ownership of assets in a relationship like ours. I'd always thought that I owned my stuff and Todd owned his, except for the business where we share everything. Then Todd said *he'd* always thought that after a while, a common-law relationship became just like a marriage and everything was owned jointly!"

"Yikes!" said Doug. "As our son Jason would say, 'Let's not go there'— or at least not over dinner. But just out of interest, and speaking hypothetically, of course, what *would* happen if one of you died?"

"There's legislation to cover what happens in the absence of a will. My lawyer said that every province has its own so-called intestate succession law."

"Intestate succession … sounds like something Viagra could fix," said Fiona, giggling and setting down her sake cup. "Okay, sorry, guys—I couldn't resist!"

"In some provinces, the intestate succession law doesn't define what is meant by a 'spouse,'" Todd continued, pretending to give Fiona the evil eye. "If you aren't considered to be legally married and you died without a will, your estate would likely go to your parents."

"And Nori would get nothing?" asked Vanessa. "Let's change the subject can we? Can't we talk about something other than dying? What I'm really interested in right now is the main course—the smells coming from the kitchen are mouth-watering."

⌒◯⌒

After the main course—miso braised beef short ribs—the group tucked into green tea pots de crème baked in Japanese tea bowls.

Nibbling on the caramelized sugar chopsticks that decorated the accompanying plates, Doug was eager to return to the earlier topic of conversation. "Todd, you mentioned that if you were to die without a will your money would go to your parents rather than to Nori. But what if your parents were no longer around?"

"The law goes to great morbid lengths as to who gets it then. First, I think, it goes to your surviving brothers or sisters, and in the event of their death, to their kids, and so on. But the point is, this intestacy stuff is just an arbitrary division and I just happen to want anything I've got to go to Nori. And the lovely Nori wants to leave everything to me, but unless we take some action, that won't happen, plain and simple."

"So what's the next step?" asked Vanessa.

"Obviously, we each have to make a will but my lawyer also thinks we should draw up a cohabitation agreement. The fact that our home is in my name but we hold the business jointly could create some problems in the future."

"Cohabitation—I've always hated that word," said Sheila. "It sounds so pompous, or something. Why can't they just say an agreement for people who live together?"

"Lawyers never seem to say anything simply," said Todd. "Although, the more I talk to them, the greater appreciation I have for what they do. Life just isn't simple or predictable, for that matter. If you'd told me that my buddy was going to be dead before he'd even reached 40, I'd have said you were crazy. One of the hardest things I have to get my head around is the need to plan just in case something might happen. I've always been a spontaneous kind of guy but I guess you can carry that only so far."

"Hey," said Vanessa. "There's nothing wrong with spontaneity. You just need to get those arrangements in place so you can forget about them and be the fun kind of person you've always been."

"I'd drink to that," said Fiona. "If only someone would give me more sake. Oops—now I've knocked my cup over! How come I'm the only one who doesn't have any?"

"Because it's time we made sure you got safely to your bed," said Vanessa. "Don't worry about your soup stuff in the kitchen—I'm going to find your jacket and get you on your way. Sayonara, Todd and Nori. Thanks for a wonderful evening—you were real troopers to go on with it after all the troubles that you've had. Good night and God bless!"

BEING AN Executor

—WHAT ME?

HAS IT HAPPENED TO YOU? Perhaps like Todd you were holding up one end of a sofa during a friend's household move, or maybe you were midway through a good family gossip session with a sister ... and then the seemingly innocuous question was asked: Will you be my executor? What are you to say? Really, isn't it an honour to be asked, and isn't there a very real chance that the will could be changed before the person dies, saving you from the whole mysterious process anyway?

SHOULD YOU AGREE TO BEING APPOINTED?

With even a little thought, you can see that it likely doesn't make sense to agree to being an executor on the off chance that you won't in fact ever be called on to act. There is a lot involved in being an executor, and it is wise to investigate the duties before you let yourself be flattered, or cajoled, into saying yes.

First of all, in doing your research, don't be confused by all the different terms. An executor is the person named in a will to administer the estate, but sometimes you will see the phrase "executor and trustee." A "trustee" refers to the person who will look after any assets that are directed in the will to be "held in trust" for a period of time, for example, until a beneficiary becomes old enough to accept the assets in the beneficiary's own name. However, it is usual for the person named as the executor to also act as the trustee of any trusts, so "executor and trustee" refers to the same person in 99% of all cases.

As well, other titles seem to have arisen over the years for the same job, such as personal representative. Don't be confused—generally all such titles are referring to the executor and trustee's role.

STAGES OF AN EXECUTOR'S JOB

There are several stages to an executor's job. The first occurs when the executor is notified of the death. In Todd's situation, he had long since forgotten that he had agreed to be Scott's executor, so the responsibility had come as a complete shock. In other cases, the executor knows that he or she has been appointed and will ideally know where the will is located.

In either case, an executor is always free to "renounce" the duty—an executor is not legally required to act as the executor if at the time of the death circumstances do not permit the executor to take on the job. The executor wishing to renounce, however, must decide to do so quickly because once an individual named as an executor starts to act, it soon becomes legally difficult to step back from the executorship role.

Once an executor named in a will has decided to take on the job, the next stage is a very busy one. The first week may mostly be spent attending to funeral arrangements. Although the executor has the legal right to make the final decisions on the funeral arrangements, the wise executor will consider the wishes that the deceased may have set out in his or her will, and the views of close relatives.

Soon after the funeral, there are typically several days or even weeks of traipsing around to the lawyer's office, one or more banks, a couple of insurance agencies, and some government offices. It is at this stage that a new executor, like Todd, can feel overwhelmed!

A couple of common sense ideas to try include lining up a meeting with a lawyer familiar with estate work, and getting your hands on a good "executor's task list." Such lists are readily available from trust companies, some law offices, and several do-it-yourself books on estate planning or being an executor. Much of the work of an executor is not difficult—the challenge lies in simply making sure it all gets done!

A meeting with a lawyer who has done a fair bit of wills and estate work can set you on the right track. This may be the same lawyer who was holding the deceased's will, or it may be someone recommended to you as an expert in the field. Don't leave the meeting until you are comfortable with two important items:

- First, understand who will be responsible for all the tasks that lie ahead.

- Second, gain at least a basic understanding of the murky area of estate costs and fees, including the compensation that the lawyer will earn, your fees as an executor, and the court's fees.

These two central issues of, first, the division of tasks and, second, compensation, are really related topics. The boundary between the lawyer's tasks and the executor's tasks can be blurry, and who takes on certain jobs affects how much each party can charge the estate. Even if you are not planning to charge for your work as an executor, it is important to realize that by asking the lawyer to assume some of the traditional executor tasks, the legal fees will be higher. This delegation of tasks may turn out to be a very prudent use of estate funds, but as executor, you need to be in control of the situation, not just going along with suggestions made by advisers along the way.

In beginning your work as an executor, try to take one step at a time, ask lots of questions, read as much as possible, and early on in the process, set up a system to keep yourself organized. Even if you do not consider yourself a really organized person, keep in mind that these are someone else's affairs you are responsible for, and there is a very real duty to cross all the *t's* and dot all the *i's*!

The right lawyer will have worked with executors on many estates and will be able to easily walk you through what at first seem like daunting issues. As an overview, it may be helpful to think of the estate administration process as involving a few distinct stages:

1. Making preliminary arrangements, such as looking after any immediate financial needs of beneficiaries;

2. Locating and securing all of the deceased's assets;

3. Assembling and affixing a value to the estate property;

4. Paying debts and bequests, and looking after tax compliance;

5. Distributing and winding up the estate.

WHO SHOULD BE YOUR EXECUTOR?

Having had your pants scared off with the story of Todd suddenly being catapulted to the status of an executor, what is the best advice for picking your executor? Like being an executor itself, the task of selecting a good executor really comes down to common sense ... whom do you trust completely? Who could you ask—at a moment's notice—to look after your house, your car, and your business, and file your tax return, and know—just know—that it would all be done, and done well? *Who is that person?*

The "Top Ten" Criteria for an Executor

For those of you who like lists, here is a "Top Ten" list to keep in mind when picking an executor:

1. Pick someone who schedules changing the smoke detector battery and pays taxes on time—you want someone who is a bit obsessive when it comes to details, deadlines, and getting things done.

2. Find a "people person." Beneficiaries can act oddly, like saying at the funeral, "Grandma always paid my telephone bill—can I get a cheque today?" An executor's work often involves some delicate situations.

3. Resist the temptation to name all your children as executors, just to avoid hurting their feelings. One, or more, will end up renouncing the role to simplify things, or else the estate will be a cumbersome operation requiring more time and expense than necessary. Talk to all of them and select the one or two children who would be good at the job.

4. Don't pick anyone who will be over 65 by the time the youngest beneficiary gets the last distribution—everyone deserves a retirement. If the trusts in your will end when your youngest child is 30, figure out how old the executor will be at that time—90? Think again.

5. Avoid naming the same person(s) to be both the guardian and the executor. It is difficult to be the guardian of a teenager who needs a Corvette to drive to school when you also happen to have control of a large trust fund. A division of labour is a good idea.

6. Try not to appoint more than three executors. Unless otherwise stated in the will, the executors must agree on everything, so a big team of executors can really bog things down and add to the overall expense.

7. Related to the above item, choose executors who are smart enough and humble enough to know when to retain good help—accountants, insurance advisers, lawyers, realtors, investment counselors. The executor's potential for significant liability can be reduced greatly if advice is obtained as needed.

8. Don't dismiss the idea of a professional executor. If, for example, your affairs are complex or controversial, or your ideal executors live out of province, at least inform yourself about this option.

9. Get permission! No one is obligated to take on the responsibility of being an executor when a person dies, but you can reduce the chance of your executor renouncing his or her appointment by getting consent ahead of time.

10. Don't abandon your will once it is completed the first time around, especially the executorship appointment. The importance of this function cannot be overstated, so reflect annually on the executor(s) named in your will.

THE *Menu*

⤜◎⤛

Yam and ginger bisque

Halibut and sweet melon ceviche with cellophane noodles

Miso braised beef short ribs, onions, and leeks

Spicy pickled cucumbers

Green tea pots de crème with burnt sugar "chopsticks"

⤜◎⤛

*Yam and ginger bisque**   SERVES 8

A brilliant, sunny, orange hue, this bisque is best presented in shallow, white soup plates with a drizzling of heavy cream or thinned crème fraîche. The "yams" used in this recipe are actually sweet potatoes. They are long and irregular in shape and have a reddish skin and coral-coloured flesh.

2	large sweet potatoes, approximately 4 ½ pounds (2 kg) in total	2
1	large onion	1
2 tbsp.	butter	25 mL
1 ½ tsp.	salt	7 mL
½ tsp.	white pepper	2 mL
1	2-inch (5 cm) piece of fresh ginger	1
4 cups	chicken stock	1 L
1 cup	milk	250 mL
1 cup	heavy cream (35% M.F.)	250 mL
	Juice of ½ lime	

1. Peel the sweet potatoes and cut them into 1-inch (2.5 cm) chunks. Cut the onion into rough dice.

2. In a stock pot or Dutch oven, over medium-high heat, melt the butter and add the sweet potatoes and onion.

3. Add the salt and white pepper and continue to cook, stirring occasionally, until the sweet potatoes are soft, approximately 10 minutes. Be careful! Because of the high sugar content of the sweet potatoes and onions, they burn easily. Turn down the temperature if necessary.

---

*Adapted from *City Cuisine*, First Edition, by Susan Feniger and Mary Sue Milliken. Copyright 1989 by William Morrow and Company, Inc.

4. Remove the pot from the burner, and grate the ginger directly into the pot. Scrape the ginger from the inside of the grater, but do not use the fibre that collects on the outside.

5. Return the pot to the burner and cook, stirring for an additional 3 minutes.

6. Add the chicken stock and scrape the bottom of the pot clean of bits of sweet potato and onion. These bits should be a nice golden brown. If they are black, you weren't paying attention during step 3!

7. Bring to a boil, reduce heat to low, and simmer, uncovered for another 10 minutes.

8. Remove the pot from the burner and purée the mixture with an immersion blender or carefully transfer the mixture to a regular blender or food processor and purée until completely smooth.

9. Return the pot to the burner or, if you've used a regular blender or food processor, return the soup to the pot first. Then add the milk and cream. Bring the soup almost to a boil, then remove it from the heat.

10. Stir in the lime juice, adjust the seasoning and serve.

Halibut and sweet melon ceviche
with cellophane noodles   SERVES 8

Ceviche

1 tbsp.	chopped coriander	15 ml
1 tbsp.	minced green onion	15 mL
1 tbsp.	minced red onion	15 mL
½ to 1	serrano chili, minced	½ to 1
	Zest and juice of two small limes	
¼ cup	peanut oil	50 mL
½ tsp.	salt	2 mL
1 pound	fresh, skinless, boneless halibut filet, cut into ½-inch (1cm) chunks	500 g
½	small, ripe cantaloupe or honeydew melon, cut into ½-inch (1cm) chunks	½
1 cup	long English cucumber, seeds scooped out and cut into ¼-inch (5mm) thick crescents	250 mL

1. In a small bowl or jar, combine coriander, green onion, red onion, serrano chili, lime zest, lime juice, peanut oil, and salt. Whisk or shake until well blended.

2. Combine halibut, melon, and lime mixture. Refrigerate 3 to 4 hours before serving. Shortly before serving, add cucumbers.

Noodles

¼ cup	rice vinegar	50 mL
¼ cup	Japanese soy sauce	50 mL
	Juice of 1 small lime	
¼ cup	peanut butter	50 mL
1 tsp.	sesame oil	5 mL
2 tbsp.	Thai fish sauce	20 mL
	Freshly ground black pepper, to taste	
4 ounces	bean thread, dry*	125 g
½ cup	coarsely chopped, roasted, salted peanuts,	125 mL
8	Sprigs of fresh coriander	8

* Cellophane noodles, also called bean thread, are a type of Chinese mung bean noodle which, when cooked, become transparent.

1. In a bowl, make a vinaigrette by whisking together the rice vinegar, soy sauce, lime juice, peanut butter, sesame oil, fish sauce, and black pepper. Set aside.

2. In a large saucepan, bring 8 cups (2 L) of water to a boil. Break the bean thread in half and add to the boiling water. Cook for 10 minutes. Rinse under cold, running water, drain, and toss with the peanut vinaigrette.

3. Curl approximately ⅔ cup (150 ml) of the noodles into each of 8 small bowls. Spoon ½ cup (125 mL) of the ceviche, with some of the marinade, over the noodles, and garnish with chopped peanuts and a sprig of fresh coriander.

Miso braised beef short ribs, onions, and leeks

Look for individual short ribs approximately 3 inches (8cm) in length. One rib per person is usually enough, but always make a few extra for those with a more hearty appetite. As with most braised dishes, this one makes great leftovers and can be made a day or two ahead, then reheated in a 375°F (190°C) oven, covered with a lid or foil.

Marinade

½ cup	sake	125 mL
½ cup	Japanese soy sauce	125 mL
¼ cup	canola oil	50 mL
3	green onions, coarsely chopped	3
3 tbsp.	sesame oil	50 mL
2	cloves garlic	2
½-inch piece	fresh ginger	1 cm piece
½ tsp.	black pepper	2 mL

Put all marinade ingredients into a blender or food processor, and process approximately 30 seconds. It doesn't matter whether the marinade contains pieces of solid material. It will be discarded before the ribs go into the oven.

Ribs

10	beef short ribs, 7 to 8 pounds (3.5 to 4 kg), in total	10
¼ cup	Japanese soy sauce	50 mL
½ cup	sake	125 mL
½ cup	light miso*	125 mL
	Freshly ground black pepper, to taste	
2 tbsp.	flour	20 mL
3 cups	beef stock	750 mL
1	large onion, sliced ¼-inch (2mm) thick	1
2 to 3	leeks, white and tender green parts only, sliced into strips ¼ inch (2mm) thick and 3 inches (8 cm) long	2 to 3
3	green onions	3

* Miso, a staple of the Japanese kitchen, is a paste made from a fermentation of soy beans. It is available in a wide range of strengths, colours, and flavours. Generally, the darker the colour of the miso, the stronger the flavour. Miso is available at Asian supermarkets and most health food stores.

1. Put short ribs into a non-reactive container (glass, stainless steel, or ceramic). Pour the marinade over the ribs, turn to coat, and refrigerate, covered, for 8 to 24 hours, turning every few hours.

2. Heat oven to 350°F (180°C).

3. In a bowl, combine soy sauce, sake, miso, black pepper, flour, and beef stock. Whisk until all lumps of flour are incorporated. Set it aside.

4. Remove the ribs from the marinade. Put the ribs and onions in one or two large, shallow baking dishes. Cover them with the miso mixture.

5. Cover the dishes with aluminum foil and bake in the oven for 1 ½ hours.

6. Remove the foil. Add the leeks and stir to blend them in. Bake another 1 to 1 ½ hours, until the meat is very tender when tested with a fork.

7. Remove the ribs to individual plates or to a serving platter. Garnish with diagonally cut or curls of green onion.

Spicy pickled cucumbers   SERVES 8

This spicy side dish was inspired by a cucumber kim chee, a variation on Korean pickled cabbage, created by Calgary chef David Hampton.

2	long English cucumbers	2
1 cup	red wine vinegar	250 mL
1 clove	garlic, minced	1 clove
2 tsp.	salt	5 mL
1 tbsp.	sambal oelek*	15 mL
½ inch	piece of ginger	1 cm

* Asian chili paste. Available in Asian markets and most supermarkets.

1. Slice the cucumbers diagonally, as thinly as possible, using a sharp serrated knife or a mandoline. Put the cucumber slices into a colander set over a bowl, and allow them to drain for about an hour, stirring occasionally.

2. In a large glass jar or bowl, combine the vinegar, garlic, salt, and sambal oelek. Grate in the ginger.

3. Add the cucumbers and marinate for at least 30 minutes.

Green tea pots de crème with burnt sugar "chopsticks"   SERVES 8

These custards are flavoured with the "Matcha" tea used in the Japanese tea ceremony. You'll find it in most Asian markets.

2½ cups	milk (not low fat)	625 mL
1 cup	heavy cream (35% M.F.)	250 mL
3	eggs	3
3	egg yolks	3
½ cup	sugar	125 mL
4 tbsp.	green tea powder	65 mL
	Pinch of salt	

1. Heat oven to 325°F (160°C). Place eight 6-ounce (175 mL) ramekins* in a shallow baking pan. Set aside.

2. In a saucepan, over medium heat, bring the milk and cream up to the boiling point, but do not allow to boil. Remove it from the heat, cover it, and let it stand at room temperature.

3. In a bowl, whisk together the eggs, egg yolks, sugar, green tea powder, and salt.

4. Gradually whisk in the hot milk and cream and strain the mixture through a fine meshed sieve into a wide-mouthed pitcher.

5. Pour the custard into the ramekins, leaving a bit of room at the top for expansion.

6. Carefully pour hot water from a kettle into the baking pan, filling it to half the depth of the ramekins. Transfer the pan to the oven and cover the tops of the ramekins with a baking sheet.

7. Bake for 40 to 50 minutes. Test for doneness by removing the baking sheet and gently tapping the edge of one of the ramekins with a spoon. If the custard is still liquid in the centre, it is not done. When it is done, it will have the approximate firmness of sour cream. Do not overbake.

8. Remove the pan from the oven and the ramekins from the pan. Allow to stand until they've reached room temperature, then transfer them to the refrigerator to chill at least 4 hours. Serve in the ramekins, on a dessert plate, with the burnt sugar "chopsticks" on the side.

* Ovenproof Japanese teacups may be used in place of the ramekins.

Burnt sugar "chopsticks"

1 cup	sugar	250 mL
1 tbsp.	lemon juice	15 mL
¼ cup	water	50 mL

1. Cover a baking sheet with parchment paper. Set aside.

2. Place all the ingredients in a small saucepan and stir them together very gently, taking care to not splash the sides of the pan. Place a shallow bowl of ice water nearby.

3. Heat the mixture over medium-high heat. Do not stir. If the inside walls of the pan become splashed with sugar, wash them down with a pastry brush dipped in fresh water.

4. Heat the sugar mixture to a dark amber colour. You don't really want to burn the sugar, but it should be darker than the colour of rye whiskey. Remove the pan from heat and immediately plunge the bottom of the

pan into the ice water to prevent the sugar from darkening further. Be very careful when working with caramelized sugar. It is extremely hot!

5. Remove the pan from the water and dry the outside. With a teaspoon, stir the sugar mixture at the bottom of the pan and slowly raise the spoon. If the mixture is very viscous and holds together for a few inches, it is ready to use. If it is still very liquid and thin, allow it to cool a few more minutes.

6. Using the teaspoon, make several 8-inch (20 cm) long "sticks" on the parchment paper. Make more than you need—some will likely break. Work as quickly as you can—as the sugar cools it will harden. Leave the chopsticks on the parchment until needed. If you are making them ahead of time, store in an airtight container, away from humidity.

Advance Preparation

Two days before the dinner:

1. Marinate short ribs.

2. Make green tea pots de crème and burnt sugar "chopsticks."

The day of the dinner:

A.M.

1. Prepare bisque through step 8.

2. Prepare spicy pickled cucumbers.

<u>P.M.</u>

1. Prepare the ceviche 4 to 5 hours before serving.

2. Braise the short ribs at least 3 hours before serving.

Shortly before the guests arrive

Steam the rice 1 hour before serving.

Restaurant FAVOURITES

"I'M WORRIED ABOUT THAT SON OF OURS," SAID SHEILA ENRIGHT AS SHE HUNG UP THE PHONE.

"What's he up to now?" asked Doug, raising his head reluctantly from the Sports section of the newspaper.

"Well, that's just it—who knows what he's up to? That must be the fifth time this week I've tried his number and he's never there. I do need to talk to him about changing the date for his flight home."

"Don't be too hard on him, Sheila. You can hardly expect him to be in his room every night—a guy's gotta live, you know."

"Of course, I don't expect him to be in his room *every* night but finals are coming up and I sure hope he's doing at least a little bit of studying."

"Maybe he's at the library," said Doug. "Burning the midnight oil and ploughing through obscure learned texts. Then again, he may be at the pub". They both burst out laughing.

"Look, Sheila, Jason'll be okay," said Doug, setting his newspaper aside and giving Sheila a quick hug. "Hey, I wasn't exactly the model student and look at me now—solid middle management, can't get more establishment than that. Just relax and send him an e-mail if you can't get in touch by phone."

"I did," said Sheila. "Three to be exact. Got any more bright ideas?"

"Yep. Let's go to bed."

❧

Sheila set off for her office the next day determined to put the matter of Jason out of her mind. It was a bright clear morning and she was looking forward to resuming her fair-weather practice of walking to work instead of catching a ride with Doug. The snow had mostly disappeared, leaving the grass on the boulevards brown and exposed. However, on the south side of an apartment building she was rewarded by the sight of a cluster of blue scilla, their fragile blooms trembling in the breeze.

Today Sheila had the kind of appointments she enjoyed—two new assessments and what would probably be her last session with a favourite client whom she had treated for the last six months. Together they had finally got his stutter under control—it was the kind of success story she'd imagined when she first went into speech pathology. Unfortunately, those kinds of results weren't always achieved despite her best efforts. Just as with Jason, she thought. Surely he'd return her messages some time soon but it probably wouldn't be until he needed something "essential"—what parent wouldn't buckle to an urgent request for required textbooks? Sheila suspected the money was actually destined to be spent at the local watering hole but, for the most part, Doug gave Jason the benefit of the doubt. Pausing at an intersection, Sheila realized she was letting her wayward son occupy her mind again. "Don't dwell on things that are only going to upset you," she told herself and then set off with renewed purpose as the light turned green.

❦

Home again at the end of the day, Sheila congratulated herself on having mostly kept Jason out of her thoughts. She was rewarded by a cheery voice-mail message from him—"Sorry you've kept missing me, Mom, but me and my buddy Ryan have been holed up going over our Psych notes." Of course, she would still have to get in touch with him to sort out his flight arrangements but at least it sounded like he had actually been doing some work. What a nice way to start the weekend, and tomorrow there was the added treat that Doug was going to wine and dine her. When he'd asked her where she'd like to go to celebrate their 20th wedding anniversary, Sheila hadn't hesitated in suggesting their favourite spot on the 4th Street restaurant strip. The menu featured only locally grown produce and meats and had quickly become Doug and Sheila's restaurant of choice.

On their last visit there to celebrate Valentine's Day, they'd asked the chef to supply them with the recipe for his rack of lamb dish, and when he graciously complied, it had given Sheila an idea. "How about asking each of our neighbours to have a chat with the chef at their favourite restaurant and get a recipe to use at our next dinner club meeting? It's our turn to host next month, you know."

"Sounds like fun," Doug had said, "but how easy would it be to get chefs to part with their recipes? Don't they think of them as privileged information, like Coca-Cola or that 'secret blend of herbs and spices?'"

"Most chefs nowadays have a pretty wide repertoire and they make different dishes all the time, depending on what's in season. It's not like they only have 10 recipes."

"That's true, and I guess if you're a regular customer they wouldn't mind doing you a favour. Why don't we run the idea by the others and see what they think?"

⁓⊙⊙⁓

Getting ready for her night out, Sheila pampered herself with a long soak in the Jacuzzi before she dressed for dinner. At times like this she didn't miss Jason yelling through the bathroom door, "Hey, Mom, what's there to eat? I'm starving!" On the other hand, she did miss Jason's exuberant good nature and she smiled at the thought of having him home for the summer months. A moment later she smiled at the thought of herself smiling. She knew darned well that after the euphoria of the first couple of days had worn off, she'd be looking back enviously at the quiet times she and Doug had enjoyed as empty nesters. Thank God, teenagers are born to rebel, she thought, otherwise, they might never leave home.

Dressed in a new silk shirt and crêpe pants Sheila walked into the kitchen where Doug was trying to tie a purple ribbon on a gift-wrapped box.

"I'm all thumbs when it comes to this stuff," said Doug. "Here, you'd better have it just the way it is."

Opening the box, Sheila discovered a bone china teacup and saucer with a hand-painted design of jonquils.

"I looked up on the Internet what the gifts are supposed to be for the various wedding anniversaries and it said china for the 20th…"

"Oh, Doug, that's so sweet of you!"

"But I didn't think that was much of a present. I got you this too."

Opening the second box, Sheila found a tiny tear-drop diamond suspended on a fine gold chain.

"Doug, it's beautiful! What a wonderful surprise—you're more romantic than when we first met!"

"Hey, the night is young, as they say! And now, your carriage—or at least your Pathfinder—awaits. Shall we go?"

⤸⊙⊚⊙⤷

Over dinner, Doug asked Sheila how plans were proceeding for the next meeting of the dinner club.

"Very well, I think," said Sheila. "Or, at least, everyone thought it was a good idea.

I guess it remains to be seen whether they all come up with recipes."

"If they do, it could be a wonderful night."

"Not as great as tonight," said Sheila, reaching across the table for Doug's hand. "Nothing could be as special as this."

⤸⊙⊚⊙⤷

Doug and Sheila decided to convene the March dinner club meeting a half hour earlier than usual. For the first time in months, there was some significant condominium business to discuss—a late spring snowfall had resulted in water seeping through the skylights in all their homes. The builder had denied responsibility saying that the damage had occurred as a result of an ice build-up that the owners could have avoided by having the roofs shovelled.

Gerald Porter opened the discussion. "I think our first step should be to get an independent inspection carried out—that's the only way we'll know for sure whether it's shoddy workmanship on the part of the builder."

"What if it turns out that the seal on the skylights is at fault—then do we have to go after the manufacturer?" asked Nori.

"All I know," said Todd, "is that we'll probably need to get a lawyer involved. My experience over the last month or so has been that they're the ones who are really running the world!"

"Oh, yes, I forgot—it's Todd the Executor, isn't it?" asked Fiona. "How are you making out?

"Well, without Scott's lawyer to point me in the right direction, I'd be a raving lunatic by now. It's a way bigger deal than I ever imagined. Every time I turn around, there's something new to deal with."

"Did your friend leave things in kind of a mess?" asked Fiona.

"No, as a matter of fact, I've learned that Scott could have made things much tougher on me. For one thing, on the advice of his lawyer, he named the estate as beneficiary of his life insurance. That has simplified matters a lot."

"Can we simplify matters with respect to the skylight issue?" asked Gerald, faced with the daunting task of keeping the meeting on track. "Shall we proceed with getting an inspection and then, based on the findings, decide what our next move should be? After all, it may turn out that neither the builder nor the manufacturer is at fault. In that case, there wouldn't be much point in getting a lawyer involved."

"Sounds good to me," said Doug. "Although, recently, I've become quite a fan of getting lawyers involved. Remind me over dinner and I'll tell you how Sheila and I could have paid a big price for *not* getting a lawyer involved."

"Don't tell me we're having a lawyers' love-in," said Fiona, laughing. "That would be a first, wouldn't it?"

"I'm not saying that no one should make a move without one but you'd better know what you're doing if you decide to go it alone. And speaking of going it alone, I'd better give Sheila a hand if you'll excuse me. I was supposed to open the wine to let it breathe and I forgot all about it. Here's hoping it can take a few deep breaths and be done with it!"

⌒⊙⌒

"Please come to the table," said Sheila. "I hope no one is allergic to hyacinth—I got a bit carried away when I saw the beautiful baskets of spring bulbs that Nori had cleverly put in her store window. I think we're all craving some kind of sign that winter is finally over."

"You'd hardly know it by looking outside today," said Vanessa. "I almost cried when I woke up this morning and saw that it was snowing again. Still it didn't last long and we can cheer ourselves up by looking at your beautiful table."

"Let's just hope the skylights don't start leaking again," said Gerald. "Oops, sorry everyone, I didn't mean to drag condo business into the fun part of the evening. Tonight's the night we get to taste the recipes from all the different chefs, isn't it?"

"So you were listening after all," said Vanessa with a smile. "I never know whether I should interpret your grunts as 'message received' or 'leave me alone, I've got reading to do.'"

"Of course I was listening," Gerald replied. "Information about food wins out over the latest treatment for myocardial infarction any day of the week."

"Sheila, I have to admit you came up with a terrific idea for tonight's theme. I love the surprise element," said Vanessa.

"Let's hope all the surprises are good and not like the one we had regarding our wills when we went to see our lawyer recently," said Sheila. "Did Doug tell you about it when I was busy in the kitchen?"

"He did bring it up but we haven't heard any of the details," said Todd. "What happened exactly?"

"As you know, we wanted to change our wills so as to leave our money in trust for Jason. We thought we'd better consult a lawyer since it seemed a lot more complicated a situation than when we first wrote our wills years ago. What we did then was purchase a couple of those kits from a stationer's and fill them out."

"I think it took us all of about 10 minutes," said Doug. "I remember it was shortly after Jason was born. We were enjoying one of our hot Saturday night dates—the latest video release and a couple of beers. Between the end of the video and the arrival of the pizza guy, we polished off our last wills and testaments and when Sheila's brother dropped by the next day, we got him to witness them."

"Excuse me for asking," said Fiona, "but is there a point to this story?"

"Yes," said Sheila. "The point is that when we went to see our lawyer, we took our wills with us only to find out that they had been invalid all along!"

"Invalid?" said Fiona. "Had you forgotten to sign them or something?"

"No, we'd done that all right. What we hadn't realized is that a will is invalid without the signature of *two* witnesses. It's hard to believe we could have been so stupid but there you are."

"Apparently it's not that uncommon," said Doug. "Sheila was ready to totally beat up on herself—and me—but our lawyer says he comes across these situations all the time. One of the biggest mistakes people make with these 'do-it-yourself' wills is they get people to witness them who are beneficiaries."

"How is that a problem?" asked Nori.

"It's a pretty big problem. If the person witnessing the will is named as a beneficiary, they are not allowed to receive their inheritance."

"No way! You mean if I witness my grandfather's will and he's leaving a gift to me, I'm out of luck?" asked Fiona.

"Yep," said Sheila. "Doesn't it just bring to mind those awful Hollywood B movies where the competing siblings are all trying to worm their way into their father's favour before the old guy croaks? I guess the law is designed to blow the whistle—you can't exert undue influence and then conceal it by witnessing the will yourself. Requiring the witness to be a disinterested party is meant to be some kind of check and balance, I suppose."

"Well, you live and learn," said Vanessa. "Here I am a grown woman—more than grown, for heaven's sakes!—and I've never heard of that before. But what really interests me is what would have happened if you had been unlucky enough to die while your wills were invalid."

"Can you hang on for just a minute?" asked Sheila. "I want to serve the lamb before it stands too long."

"I'll help clear the dishes," said Doug. "Todd, would you do the honours by pouring the wine—I'm guessing it's done all the breathing it needed to do. Thanks, pal!"

∽⊙∾

The lamb brought with it a scent of rosemary—indeed, each plate had a pretty green sprig on it. This set off a lively discussion on the reason for this common practice.

"Setting aside the question of whether herbs are used for taste or merely for eye-appeal, I'd love to go back to what we were talking about earlier, Sheila. If you and Doug had gotten mown down by a bus on the way to the video store, what would have happened to Jason?" asked Fiona.

"That was my first thought," said Sheila. "There was an idea tucked at the back of my mind that a child in those circumstances would be taken by the state. Probably something I'd picked up watching too much American TV in my youth. It turns out that the day-to-day care of the child would be assumed by whomever the court thinks is in the child's best interests—usually a family member. In our case, we'd already asked my brother and he and his wife had agreed to act as guardians, so that's probably the way it would have turned out."

"What about your assets?" asked Fiona. "Would the government have got its hands on those?"

"Not in the sense of confiscating them, or anything draconian like that," said Doug. "No, our lawyer explained that our estate would have been held in trust by the Public Trustee and appropriate expenditures would have been paid out for Jason's upbringing. Then, when he reached the age of 18, he would have received everything as his inheritance."

"Just what you went to the lawyer to prevent!" said Fiona. "There's a certain irony in that, isn't there?"

"You can say that again," said Doug. "The foolish thing is that we went all those years thinking we had everything in place, except of course, we didn't. It's tempting to look back and say, 'Oh, well, where's the harm? We *didn't* get knocked down by a bus so what did it matter in the end?' But people would think you were nuts if you drove without car insurance for 20 years and then congratulated yourself on never having had an accident. The point is, getting your estate planning in order is far too important a matter to take a chance on."

"Does it mean you *have* to go to a lawyer to be sure you have a valid will?" asked Nori.

"Well, I guess not," Sheila replied. "If you didn't have any complicating issues and you got one of those blank forms and filled it out correctly, and confirmed it was valid in your province, *and* got it properly witnessed, I guess you'd be fine but the point is, you'd never know for sure, would you?"

"I've often wondered about those, whad'ya call em, holographic wills," said Todd.

"They're always a big item in those B movies, too. You know, the old geezer's in bed, the curtains are drawn, he picks up a quill pen and starts scratching away on a piece of parchment. It's like they never heard of ball-point pens!"

"I think they *can* be legal," said Doug, "but you'd have to really know what you're doing. Funnily enough, I think that if a will is totally written by hand, not using any typed words at all, then it doesn't require the two witnesses that a stationer's form needs. Pretty weird, eh?"

"You've got that right," said Sheila. "But apart from making sure that you've dotted all the i's and crossed all the t's, I think it really does make sense to go to a professional. There were all sorts of issues related to setting up the trust for Jason that I wouldn't have imagined in a million years."

"Sheila's right," said Doug. "Over the past year, I've developed quite a bit of respect for what they do. Just look at us—we've all benefited from getting good advice. I sort of think about it this way—if our light switch goes on the blink, I probably know enough about electricity to fix it. On the other hand, what I *don't* know might be enough to kill me. There is such a thing as false economy!"

"Now there's a cheerful note to end on!" said Fiona. "How about I serve my dessert and we can have a wee change of subject?"

❧

"Fiona—this presentation is fantastic. For someone who hasn't cooked much, I'm truly impressed. Where did you get the idea of placing the fresh rose on top?"

"Oh, hush, Vanessa. You're making me feel self-conscious. It was nothing, really—nothing that anyone here couldn't have done."

"I'm not sure I would agree with that," said Doug. "If you'd like me to serve it, I'd be honoured."

Plate after plate of Fiona's delicious Dacquoise went around the table until all were served and the picking up of forks could begin. Within minutes, Todd waved his fork, and asked for more. "This is so good, it's like a professional made it."

"All right, all right, I confess," said Fiona, blushing to the roots of her curly red hair. "The recipe didn't seem too difficult but I had a total disaster in the kitchen when I tried to make it. The lemon curd turned out just fine but I couldn't get the meringues to harden properly. So there I was on the phone to the bakery first thing this morning and by luck they were able to whip one up for me. But then I was horrified to see how professional it looked. I never thought you'd believe I'd made it in a million years. I actually considered sort of messing it up but that did seem silly."

Doug began to laugh. "You know, I *wondered* about this cardboard base under the dessert. I imagined you'd really gone over the top in your effort to make it look authentic!"

"Who cares who made it?" said Vanessa. "It's absolutely delicious regardless of whose kitchen it came from."

"So, you're not going to fire me from the Dinner Club?" asked Fiona. "I was hoping I'd be able to bluff my way through but I guess I'm not made that way."

Gerald raised his glass in a toast. "Here's to many more of Fiona's delicious 'home-made' desserts!"

THE *Trouble with*

DO-IT-YOURSELF WILLS

SIMPLE AND INEXPENSIVE, WHAT COULD BE BETTER? You don't want the trouble and expense of seeing a lawyer, so why not listen to the ads for will kits on the television, or go onto the Internet, and just look after that tedious task of estate planning all on your own?

There are several good reasons why this doesn't make sense, some of which were discussed over dinner at the Elderberry Gate Dinner Club's March party.

THE TROUBLE WITH DO-IT-YOURSELF WILLS

Technical Glitches...

As Doug and Sheila's will-making experience showed the group, the most basic issue with do-it-yourself wills is that they can so easily have technical errors. Unfortunately, these technical errors usually render a will invalid.

Doug and Sheila used a so-called "stationer's form" (in more recent years, these fill-in-the-blank things have been advertised as "will kits" and can be found on the Internet) and the mistake they made was to sign them in the presence of only one witness. Rules about signing wills can vary somewhat from one province to another, but wills usually require at least two witnesses.

As well, to further complicate matters, both witnesses must be there together at the time that the person signs his or her will, and then each witness must also stick around for the other witness to sign the document.

This all sounds fairly nitpicky, but the law wants to separate what "may" be a will from what is really a will, and it has always been assumed that one way to achieve that goal is to ensure a strict practice is in place for will execution (a fancy term for will signing).

More Substantive Dilemmas...

Even if a will document is signed properly, many problems arise each year because of the content of wills. A simple example may illustrate this point.

Let's say that you and your spouse each write out a will giving $5,000 to each of your nieces and nephews, with the rest of each person's estate going first to the surviving spouse, and then to a charity, if both spouses are dead. Sounds good, but let's look more closely at the intention to give something to nieces and nephews.

If only one spouse dies, should the phrase "my nieces and nephews" be interpreted to mean only the children of the deceased's own siblings, or both the children of his or her siblings *and* the surviving spouse's siblings?

And here is another question, using the same example. If the couple perish together in an accident, did they intend each niece and nephew to receive $5,000 from each of their estates—a total of $10,000—or just one gift of $5,000? If this sounds trivial, what if the sums involved are not $5,000 and $10,000, but many hundreds of thousands?

This example is just that—only one example. The interpretation questions that can arise when a will is drafted by a person filling in the blanks in a will kit is limited only by the number of people who attempt the practice! And this point needs to be stated: The person filling out a will kit or stationer's form is likely very astute in his or her own field of endeavour, which may include engineering, medicine, or the arts. Rest assured the problems in will drafting that arise regularly are rarely, if ever, due to the will-maker's lack of smarts! The simple reality is that a significant body of knowledge and experience is applied each and every time a lawyer sits down to turn a client's will instructions into a solid and effective will. Subtleties exist in even a vanilla-flavoured will.

Of course there are many court cases that have interpreted will drafting questions, and so it certainly is fair to argue that ambiguities in a will can ultimately be resolved by litigation. Or, if your estate is lucky, resolution can occur if the group of people who "may" be your beneficiaries decide among themselves to be civil and settle the matter, more or less amicably.

But, if a compromise settled out of court is the best-case scenario, you have to ask yourself: What have you possibly gained by short-circuiting the proper preparation of a will?

And Even More Complex Issues ...

Finally, let's assume your own will is neither flawed by improper signing procedures nor worded in an ambiguous manner. You still may be subjecting your estate—and, so, your beneficiaries—to a less than ideal result.

Will drafting is like any other area of expertise—cooking, technology, tailoring garments, or repairing cars—there are always new developments and new and better techniques coming along. For example, as tax laws change, experienced wills lawyers learn, through reading and attending courses, better ways to draft wills. These new strategies may save the estate and the beneficiaries' families significant tax. Nuances like this are simply not covered in a form will leaving everything to the spouse, or else to the kids.

Again, **why shortchange your beneficiaries when a little extra time, attention, and money would result in a topnotch, professional estate plan?**

AND IF YOUR WILL IS INVALID, THEN WHAT?

Let's look at what would have happened if, as Vanessa dared to ask, Doug and Sheila had been "mown down" by a bus before the problem with their will was discovered and fixed.

The official term when a person dies without a valid will is that he or she has died intestate. Rocket science then suggests that the resulting estate mess is called an intestacy.

Intestate Estates

The law about intestate estates is based on provincial legislation, so each province has its own little differences. However, the broad brush principles are fairly similar across the country, and an intestate estate is always more hassle than an estate administered under a good will.

The primary thing that every intestacy statute tries to do is impose an arbitrary division of a deceased person's estate when that person did not leave a valid will. In itself, this intention makes sense since a person's assets have to go somewhere, and it would be chaos to think that each and every intestate estate would be divided up in a different fashion.

Those broad-brush principles mentioned above are as follows. No matter what, any debts payable at the person's death are paid first, before any distribution is made.

Then, if you die leaving no spouse and no children, your parents take everything you own, and if you have no parents surviving you, the estate is divided among your siblings, and if a sibling is dead, then his or her children take that sibling's share, and so on and so forth. More and more remote relatives are searched out if the obvious next of kin are all dead. (Ultimately, if absolutely no next of kin can be found, some part of the "Crown"—i.e., the government—will receive the estate.)

If you die leaving a spouse and no children, the spouse takes all of your property. If you die leaving a spouse and children, a specific share of your assets goes to your spouse (the exact share depends on the particular provincial legislation), and the rest is divided in a specified manner among the spouse and the children.

So what happens when a married couple dies together?

A combination of the applicable provincial legislation on intestacy and on "survivorship" applies.

Survivorship legislation simply tells us what should be assumed if two people die together in circumstances making it uncertain which of them died first. In some provinces, for example, the survivorship legislation says that the deaths are deemed to have occurred in the order of seniority—in other words, the oldest person in a married couple will be deemed to have died first.

If the couple has children together, it doesn't really matter which is deemed to have died first—all the estate will go to those children in equal shares.

However, the matter gets complicated and possibly unfair if the couple either has no children, or one or both have children that are not the children of the other spouse. (This latter possibility would arise, of course, where either or both people have children from a previous relationship.)

In either case, the oldest spouse is deemed to have died first, leaving everything to the younger person, who then is deemed to have died second, and leaving everything to his or her family. That younger person's family may be his or her parents or, as mentioned, children from an earlier relationship. Either way, it not likely that the couple would have wanted the younger person's family to inherit all the assets of both spouses.

It is crucial to remember that the specific technicalities of the distribution and administration of an intestate estate depend on the province where the deceased people lived, but whatever the jurisdiction, intestacy results in an awkward and lengthy process at best, and a legal nightmare in the worst-case situation.

As well, an intestacy

- Robs the deceased person of having a place to state wishes regarding the guardianship of minor children;

- Does not allow for token gifts to friends or the distribution of cherished personal effects, bequests to charities, and other "trivial" matters commonly addressed in a good will;

- Almost always results in higher legal fees and taxes;

- Directs that the portion of the estate going to minor children is held in trust (by the public trustee's office) only until such children reach adulthood. Very few parents willingly sign wills stipulating that their children will receive their entire inheritance upon merely becoming a adult. Depending on the province, adulthood is reached as young as 17, a sharp contrast to the usual age when people want their children to receive their inheritances, usually around 25, 30, or even older!

THE BOTTOM LINE

The bottom line is that there are indeed legally effective alternatives to a will prepared by an expert. These include will kits and forms, some even downloaded from a Web site and handwritten wills in some provinces. But several pitfalls await even a careful, well-intended layperson who is writing out a will alone. Falling into even one of those traps can result in a wholly invalid will, leaving your estate in a mess called an intestacy.

The best advice remains to set aside sufficient time, early on in your adult life, and at regular intervals throughout your life, to discuss your estate planning goals and objectives with a recommended wills lawyer. In the long run, the time and money you invest in this activity will be well spent.

THE *Menu*

༺১৩৫৯

Shrimp ravioli in leek broth with warm salsa fresca

Fresh fennel, pink grapefruit, and watercress salad

Roasted garlic cream biscuits

Grilled lamb chops with mustard oil

Cassoulet with pancetta and roasted butternut squash

Lemon white chocolate Dacquoise

༺১৩৫৯

Shrimp ravioli in leek broth with warm salsa fresca   SERVES 8

Shrimp ravioli

Instead of fresh sheet pasta, won ton wrappers are used in this recipe. They are very easy to work with and are readily available, either fresh or frozen, in most supermarkets.

1 lb	raw shrimp, shells on	500 g
1	egg	1
1	egg yolk	1
3	large shallots, finely chopped	3
2	green onions, finely chopped	2
½ tsp.	salt	2 mL
¼ tsp.	freshly ground black pepper	1 mL
1 package	won ton wrappers	1 package

1. Shell and de-vein the shrimp, reserving the shells.

2. With a large, sharp knife, chop the shrimp into pea-sized pieces.

3. Mix the shrimp with the whole egg and yolk, shallots, green onions, and salt and pepper.

4. Lay out 24 of the won ton wrappers and place 1 teaspoon (5 mL) of the filling on the centre of each. With a pastry brush dipped in water, wet the edges of six wrappers and place another wrapper squarely on top, smoothing down the edges as you go. Repeat with the remainder of the ravioli, working with approximately six at a time.

5. Bring a large pot of cold water to a rolling boil, then add 1 teaspoon (5 mL) of salt. Gently slide half of the ravioli into the water and boil 1 to 3 minutes, until the pasta has softened slightly, but is still chewy. Drain well. (If you are not using them immediately, run cold water over the ravioli and drain well. Toss them with oil and store them in an airtight container, in the refrigerator.)

Leek broth

1 tbsp.	butter	15 mL
	Shrimp shells from the ravioli	
2	leeks, roughly chopped into	2
	1-inch (2.5 cm) pieces, then washed	
1 tsp.	cracked, black peppercorns	5 mL
2 quarts	chicken stock	2 L
	Salt	
	Ground white pepper	

1. In a large saucepan, melt the butter over high heat and add the shrimp shells. Cook, stirring constantly, until shells are golden brown and beginning to smoke.

2. Add the leeks and cracked peppercorns. Reduce heat to medium.

3. When the leeks are tender, add the chicken stock. Simmer (just below boiling) for 30 minutes.

4. Strain through a sieve lined with two layers of cheesecloth. Season, to taste, with salt and white pepper.

Warm salsa fresca

1 lb.	fresh, ripe tomatoes	500 g
1 clove	garlic, minced	1 clove
1½ tsp.	fresh lime juice *	7 mL
1 tbsp.	extra virgin olive oil	15 mL
1 tbsp.	chopped, fresh basil	15 mL
	Salt and freshly ground black pepper	

* If you don't have a lime, omit this ingredient. Do not use commercially bottled lime juice.

1. Cut the tomatoes into ½-inch (1 cm) dice.

2. Combine all the ingredients in a small, non-reactive (stainless steel or glass) saucepan. Heat the sauce through without cooking the tomatoes. Season with salt and pepper, to taste.

Assembly

1	leek	1
8 cups	leek broth	2 L
24	shrimp ravioli	24
½ cup	warm salsa fresca	125 mL

1. Remove the outer layer of the leek. Cut off the tough, green top and about 1/2 inch (1 cm) off the bottom. Cut it in half, lengthwise. Slice the halves into slivers, 2 inches by ⅛ inch (5 cm by 3 mm). Put the leek slivers into a colander and wash them well.

2. Heat a non-stick skillet over medium-high heat. Add the leeks and 2 tablespoons (25 mL) of broth. Cook until the leeks are tender, but not limp, approximately 1 minute. Set aside.

3. Heat the leek broth in a saucepan over medium heat. When it's hot, add the ravioli and simmer for 2 to 5 minutes, until the ravioli are heated through.

4. Overlap three ravioli in the centre of each of eight warmed soup plates. Ladle in enough broth to cover the ravioli by two-thirds. Add 1 tablespoon (15 mL) of the leeks into each soup plate, distributing them evenly throughout the broth.

5. Spoon a heaping teaspoonful of the warm salsa on top of the ravioli. Serve.

Fresh fennel, pink grapefruit, and watercress salad   SERVES 8

Fresh fennel, sometimes called anise, can be found in most supermarkets. The bulb has the crisp texture and consistency of celery, with a mild flavour of licorice. The feathery leaves can be used as a herb or a garnish.

3	large pink grapefruit	3
1 bulb	fresh fennel	1 bulb
2 bunches	watercress (if you aren't able to find watercress, use any baby lettuce or the hearts of butter lettuce)	2 bunches
¼	red onion	¼

For the vinaigrette:

2 tbsp.	white wine vinegar or the brine from pickled red onions, page 211	25 mL
4 tbsp.	fresh grapefruit juice	60 mL
¾ cup	peanut oil	175 mL
½ tsp.	dry mustard	2 mL
	Pinch of sugar	
	Salt	
	Freshly ground black pepper	

1. Peel the grapefruit, then section it, removing all of the membrane and bitter white pith. Set aside the segments and squeeze the juice from any flesh remaining on the peel into a separate container.

2. Trim the entire green stalk off the top of the fennel bulb. Trim ¼ inch (5 mm) off the bottom. Wash and dry the bulb. Cut it into long, narrow slices, 3 inches by ¼ inch (8 cm by 5 mm). The smaller pieces in the centre will be attached to the heart. Leave them on, as this adds visual interest is delicious.

3. Remove the tougher, lower stems from the watercress and wash.

4. Thinly slice the red onion.

5. Combine the ingredients for the vinaigrette in a glass jar and shake it vigorously.

6. In a large bowl, combine the fennel, watercress, and red onion. Dress them with approximately ½ cup (125 mL) of the vinaigrette and mix to coat. Gently fold in the grapefruit segments and serve in glass bowls or mounded in the centre of large plates.

Roasted garlic cream biscuits   MAKES 1 ½ DOZEN BISCUITS

2 cups	all-purpose flour	500 mL
4 tsp.	cream of tartar	2 mL
4 tsp.	baking powder	20 mL
½ tsp.	salt	2 mL
½ cup	cold butter, cut into ½ inch (1 cm) pieces	125 mL
1 bulb	garlic, roasted (see page 30)	1 bulb
1	egg	1
Approximately ½ cup heavy cream (35% M.F.)		125 mL

1. Heat oven to 400ºF (200ºC).

2. In a large bowl, combine the dry ingredients.

3. Add the butter and squeeze the soft flesh of the garlic into the mixture. With a pastry blender or your fingertips, work in the butter and garlic until the mixture resembles coarse meal, with some pea-sized pieces.

4. In a measuring cup, lightly beat the egg, and add enough cream to total ¾ cup (175 ml). Mix well.

5. Pour the egg mixture into the flour mixture, and stir it with a fork until the liquid is mostly, but not fully, incorporated.

6. Turn the dough out onto a lightly floured countertop and with a rolling pin, roll to ½ inch (1 cm) thickness. Visualize the dough being divided into thirds, and fold each of the outer thirds over top of the centre third. This is called a three fold. Roll out the dough to ½ inch (1 cm) thickness, turn it 90 degrees, and give it another three fold. As

you are working the dough, loosen it from the countertop with a pastry scraper and dust the countertop lightly with flour, to prevent the dough from sticking. Roll out the dough to ½ inch (5 cm) thickness and cut into 2 ½-inch (6 cm) rounds with a biscuit cutter. Don't re-roll the scraps. Bake them and have them for a snack.

7. Place the rounds 1 inch (2.5 cm) apart on an ungreased baking sheet. Bake for approximately 20 minutes, until the tops and bottoms are barely golden. Transfer from the baking sheet to cooling racks.

Grilled lamb chops with mustard oil SERVES 8

Mustard oil

1 tsp	mustard seeds	5 mL
1 cup	canola oil	250 mL
1 tbsp.	dry mustard powder	15 mL
½ tsp.	garlic powder*	2 mL
1 tbsp.	white wine	15 mL

* Don't be tempted to use fresh garlic. This oil steeps at room temperature, and fresh garlic could encourage bacteria growth.)

1. Heat the mustard seeds, and 1 tablespoon (15 ml) of the oil in a small sauté pan until the mustard seeds are fragrant and popping. Remove from heat. Add the mustard powder, garlic powder, and white wine. Stir to form a paste.

2. Put the mustard mixture into a glass jar and add the remaining oil. Cover the jar and shake it well.

3. Store the jar at room temperature for 2 days and shake it often.

4. After 2 days, allow the solids to settle to the bottom of the jar and ladle the oil into a clean bottle. Store refrigerated or at room temperature.

Lamb chops

2 cloves	garlic, minced	2 cloves
⅓ cup	mustard oil	75 mL
1 tsp.	salt	5 mL
½ tsp.	freshly ground pepper	2 ml
5	racks of lamb*	5

* Have your butcher "french" the racks. The fat caps will be removed, along with the tough connective tissues, and the upper portion of the bones will be cleaned of all meat and fat.

1. Heat the oven to 375ºF (190ºC).

2. Combine the garlic, 2 tablespoons (25 mL) of mustard oil, salt, and pepper in a small bowl.

3. Rub the oil mixture onto the meat of the racks of lamb.

4. Stand the racks of lamb on a baking sheet with the bones upright. You will need to lean them into one another, forming arches.

5. Roast in the oven for approximately 15 minutes, until blue rare. Cool. (You may prepare the lamb to this point up to 1 day in advance. Be sure to cool the racks completely before refrigerating them).

6. Cut the racks into individual ribs. Just prior to serving, heat an indoor or outdoor grill until very hot. Lay each rib flat on the grill, season with salt and freshly ground pepper, and grill approximately 1 minute on each side, until each rib is cooked to medium rare and has dark, even grill marks. Place four or five ribs on each plate, atop a portion of cassoulet, and drizzle with 2 tablespoons (25 mL) of mustard oil.

Cassoulet with pancetta and roasted butternut squash

SERVES 8 TO 12

Cassoulet is originally from the Languedoc region of south-central France, and its traditional preparation is an elaborate and dogmatic affair. In 1966 the États Généraux de la Gastronomie française decreed that cassoulet must have the following proportions: 30% pork, mutton, or confit of game fowl, and 70% navy beans, stock, fresh pork rinds, herbs, and seasonings. Here we've taken some obvious liberties with this formula, with nonetheless delectable results.

2 cups	dried, white, pea beans or navy beans	500 mL
½ lb.	pancetta*, in one piece	250 g
2 cloves	garlic, minced	2
1	large onion, diced	1
2 cups	butternut squash, cut into small dice	500 mL
	Olive oil	
1 cup	chopped bitter greens	250 mL
	(chicory, kale, rapini, or mustard greens)	
3 cups	chicken, veal, or pork stock	750 mL
1 cup	dry white wine	250 mL

2	large, ripe tomatoes or 1 cup (250 mL) canned, diced tomatoes	2
½ tsp.	dried thyme	2 mL
1	bay leaf	1

* Pancetta is a type of Italian cured pork available in Italian markets and many supermarket delis.

1. Soak the beans overnight in cold water.

2. Cut the pancetta into small dice. Put the pancetta, half of the garlic, and the onion into a large cast iron casserole or Dutch oven. Set it over medium-high heat and stir until the onions are soft and transparent.

3. Drain the beans and add them to the pot. Add 8 cups (2 L) of cold water and 1 tablespoon (15 mL) of salt. Bring to a boil and skim off the foam that forms on top. Turn down the heat and simmer, uncovered, for 2 hours.

4. Heat oven to 375°F (190°C).

5. Meanwhile, toss the butternut squash with 1 teaspoon (5 mL) of olive oil, and some salt and pepper. Spread the squash in a single layer on a baking sheet and place in the oven. Roast the squash until golden brown and tender. Set aside.

6. Reduce the oven temperature to 350°F (180°C).

7. Heat 1 teaspoon (5 mL) of oil in a skillet over medium-high heat. Cook the greens for 2 minutes. Season with salt and pepper and set aside.

8. Drain the beans, reserving the cooking liquid. Return the beans to the pot and add the stock, wine, tomatoes, remaining garlic, thyme, and bay leaf. Bring it to a boil, then put the pot in the oven. Cook for 1½ to 2 hours. If the liquid evaporates before the beans are tender, add some of the original cooking liquid.

9. When the beans are soft and tender, stir in the butternut squash and the greens. Serve piping hot. (The cassoulet can be prepared through step 8 up to 3 days ahead. To serve, reheat, covered, in a 375°F (190ºC) oven. When very hot (after 45 to 60 minutes), stir in the butternut squash and greens. Return it to the oven for 5 minutes.)

Lemon white chocolate Dacquoise   SERVES 8 TO 10

Traditionally, the meringue layers in a Dacquoise are made with hazelnuts. Almonds, however, provide a subtler flavour.

Almond meringue rounds

3 ounces	sliced almonds	75 g
9	egg whites	9
1 ½ cups	sugar	375 mL

1. Heat oven to 350°F (180°C).

2. Trace a 9-inch (23 cm) circle onto each of three pieces of parchment paper. Place the parchment on three baking sheets.

3. Spread the almonds on a baking sheet and toast them in the oven until golden, not brown, approximately 5 to 7 minutes. Remove them from the oven, cool, and pulse them in a food processor until coarsely ground. Lower the oven temperature to 200°F (90°C).

4. Over low heat, simmer about 1 inch (2.5 cm) of water in a small saucepan. With an electric hand mixer, combine the egg whites and the sugar in a glass or stainless steel bowl set on the saucepan. Whip the egg whites and sugar until the mixture is very warm to the touch. Remove it from the heat, wipe the condensation from the bottom, and continue to beat the mixture until it becomes shiny and white and holds a firm peak.

5. Gently fold ¾ cup (175 mL) of the ground almonds into the meringue.

6. Spread the meringue ⅜ inch (1 cm) thick onto the parchment rounds. (Hold the parchment in place by dabbing a small amount of the meringue under the parchment, at the corners.) The rounds should be of uniform thickness and perfectly round. If you have leftover meringue, spread it in flat sections on the bare spaces of parchment. These pieces can be used as garnish.

7. Bake for about 4 hours, until the meringues are thoroughly dry and crisp. Cool them and peel off the parchment.

Lemon white chocolate mousse

9 ounces	white chocolate	255 g
1½ cups	heavy cream (35% M.F.)	375 mL
	Juice of ½ lemon	

1. Chop the chocolate and put it in a glass or ceramic bowl, along with ⅓ cup (75 mL) of the cream. Microwave it on medium in 1 minute increments, stirring after each (careful—white chocolate burns easily). When the chocolate is almost fully melted, remove it from the microwave oven and allow it to sit at room temperature, stirring occasionally, until fully melted. Add the fresh lemon juice and stir well to incorporate. Cool to room temperature.

2. Whip the remaining cream to soft peaks. Mix one-third of the whipped cream into the chocolate mixture. Fold in the rest of the cream and refrigerate for 30 minutes before using.

Lemon curd

This recipe, generously shared by Rosemary Harbrecht of Brulée Bakery in Calgary, makes perfect lemon curd, every time. It works equally well with lime juice!

¾ cup	sugar	175 mL
3	eggs	3
5 ounces	butter, melted	150 g
¾ cup	fresh lemon juice	175 ml
	Grated zest of 2 lemons	

1. In a food processor, combine the sugar and eggs.

2. Add the butter and blend well.

3. Add the juice and zest and blend well.

4. Pour the mixture into a large glass bowl and microwave it on high for a total of about 5 minutes, whisking vigorously every minute. Stop cooking when the lemon curd is as thick as pudding.

Assembly

3	9-inch (23 cm) almond meringue rounds	3
1	recipe lemon white chocolate mousse	1
½ cup	recipe lemon curd	125 mL

1. Place a spoonful of lemon white chocolate mousse on a flat cake plate, then centre one of the meringue rounds on the plate. (The mousse will hold the Dacquoise in place.)

2. Spread one-third of the mousse onto the meringue round, spreading it all the way to the edge.

3. Spread half the lemon curd onto the mousse. Top with the second meringue round.

4. Repeat.

5. Spread the remaining third of the mousse in an even, smooth layer on the top of the Dacquoise. Refrigerate up to 6 hours. Decorate with fresh flowers, crystallized flowers or petals, white chocolate curls, or pieces of broken meringue.

Advance Preparation

Two days before the dinner:

Make the cassoulet, the almond meringue rounds, and the mustard oil.

The day before the dinner:

1. Make the leek broth and the shrimp ravioli.

2. Prepare the lamb through step 5.

3. Make and chill the lemon curd.

The day of the dinner:

A.M.

1. Roast the garlic for the biscuits.

2. Prepare all the ingredients for the salad, storing them in separate containers in the refrigerator.

3. Put all the ingredients for the salsa fresca into a bowl. Do not heat.

4. Cut the leeks for the broth and put them in an airtight container. Do not refrigerate, as they will cause everything in your refrigerator to smell and taste like leeks.

P.M.

1. Make the roasted garlic cream biscuits and the lemon white chocolate mousse.

2. Assemble and decorate the Dacquoise.

Shortly before the guests arrive

An hour before dinner, put the cassoulet into the oven and cut the lamb racks into chops. Heat the leek broth and the salsa, and sauté the leeks.

Victoria Day

GARDEN PARTY

VANESSA PUT DOWN HER TROWEL AND REACHED FOR ANOTHER FLAT OF PANSIES.

"I wonder if Queen Victoria ever imagined that a hundred years after her death, people would be celebrating her birthday by getting down on their knees and rooting around in the dirt?"

"Well, I'm not paying anyone homage by getting down on my knees," said Nori. "I thought this was just the plain old 'May long weekend holiday, nowadays."

"I guess you're right," said Vanessa. "When I was a little girl we sang 'God Save the King' not 'O Canada,' and the roll-down map on the classroom wall showed all the countries in red that belonged to the British Commonwealth. Things have certainly changed … and no doubt for the better."

"How's that planter mix holding out over there, ladies?" asked Doug, who along with Todd was digging a hole to plant a small tree on the eastern edge of their communal property.

"Just fine," answered Sheila. "Why do you ask?"

"I've just remembered I was supposed to pick up some bone meal to get this tree off to a good start. I guess I'll have to make a brief pit-stop at the garden store so I was wondering if there's anything else we need."

"Brief stop?" said Sheila. "You'll be lucky. This is probably the busiest weekend of the year. Just how badly do you need that bone meal stuff?"

"The guy at the nursery said it was kind of important. I guess we *could* plant the tree today and then add the bone meal later but I think you're supposed to add it to the roots. Could be tricky once it's planted!"

"How about zipping over to your mom's and seeing whether she's got any? She's hardly going to pack up her gardening supplies for her move back east."

"Hey, smart thinking, Sheila! I'll head over there right now."

"I didn't know that Doug's mom was moving," said Vanessa as Doug backed the car out of the driveway. "Isn't she getting on a bit to be pulling up stakes?"

"That's what I thought, at first," Sheila replied. "But actually it seems to make a lot of sense. Her sister, Doug's aunt Isobel, just lost her husband. She's decided to sell their duplex in Montreal and move permanently to their cottage in the Eastern Townships. She wrote to Doug's mom asking whether she'd consider moving with her, not only for the company but also from a cost point of view—you know, it *is* a bit crazy for two widowed sisters to live at opposite ends of the country, each maintaining the cost of a household."

"There's a certain wisdom in that," said Vanessa as she stood back to admire the effect of an urn Nori had planted with pendulous begonias. "But it will be an enormous adjustment for Doug's mom, won't it?"

"Maybe, but she's really looking forward to life in the country. I think she fancies herself as a bit of a Madame Benoît—you know, raising a few lambs and growing all their veggies."

"I guess her health must be pretty good," said Fiona. "Aren't you worried about the future, though?"

"Yes," said Sheila. "She's as fit as a fiddle now but we're both a bit concerned. However, she's very determined so we've pretty much had to come to terms with her decision. Isobel's grown-up kids are pretty close by—one even lives in Cowansville—so it's not like there won't be anyone around to help them out."

"Sounds like a pretty idyllic retirement," said Vanessa. "I still keep wondering what Gerald and I will end up doing. Right now he shows no signs of easing off a bit with his practice but he can't keep going forever."

"He'll probably be one of those guys who wakes up one morning and says, 'Okay, that's it. I've had enough,'" said Fiona. "In my case, I agonized for months over whether I was doing the right thing and whether I'd have enough money to support myself for the rest of my life. Must be my Scottish ancestry, I suppose!"

"Is it your Scottish ancestry that's causing us to plant all this heather?" asked Sheila.

"No," said Fiona. "Not at all. I thought they were very nice plants and, besides, they were on special at the garden centre."

"I rest my case," said Sheila, laughing.

⋐⊙⊙⋑

When the residents of Elderberry Gate had first moved in, the consensus had been that they should hire a professional to augment the token landscaping provided by the builder. It had been Vanessa who had convinced them otherwise. "If we go with some gardening service, we'll end up with what everyone else has—a couple of spireas, impatiens in the shady areas, and some nasty two-tone petunias in pots. We could do a much better job ourselves, probably for a lot less money. Tell you what—let's do it on the

Sunday of the May long weekend. Gerald and I will have you all over for drinks afterwards."

And so it had happened, at least for the first two years. But then the other residents had convinced Vanessa that they would like to contribute some food items and the event had become one of the regular dinner club meetings.

"With one exception," said Nori. "I vote we always hold it at Gerald and Vanessa's—their location at the south end of the terrace and the fact they've got the biggest patio means they're stuck with us forever!"

This year it looked like the gardening gods were smiling on their collective endeavours.

Doug returned, bone meal in hand, the tree was manoeuvred into place, a row of spectacular large-leafed hostas were planted along the north wall, and the first cheeky dandelions of the season were surgically removed from the front lawn by Gerald. By four o'clock, the patio was swept clean and everyone had departed to freshen up for the party.

⁂

Before too long, all the residents of Elderberry Gate had assembled on the Porters' warm south-facing patio. A selection of tantalizing hors d'oeuvres was spread out on a mosaic-topped table. "After all that work, I'm starving," said Todd as he pushed a lime wedge into the narrow neck of a Corona beer. "What is there to eat?"

"Sounds like the constant refrain in our house now that Jason's back," said Sheila with a laugh.

"Oh yes," said Vanessa. "I saw Jason the other day with some of his pals —every one of them with a slice of pizza in hand. They were climbing into one of those Jeep things with roll bars and skateboard bumper stickers."

"That would be the little run-about owned by his good friend, Casey —who, it seems, doesn't have to work at all this summer, other than on improving his golf game and getting a tan. Of course, since we're the bad, mean parents, we insisted on Jason getting a job. Much to our surprise, he actually got one! Even better, it's at a restaurant and he can buy food there at staff prices. I think he also likes to 'help out' when the chef has a bit of a disaster in the kitchen. One thing you can say for him is that he's definitely without discrimination when it comes to food!"

"Whereas the rest of us here at Elderberry Gate have the most discriminating of tastes," said Nori. "Just take a look at that spread before Todd becomes a one-man wrecking crew." Surveying the spread—smoked salmon corn cakes, a savoury cheesecake, pita chips and crackers, onion and mushroom squares, an assortment of vegetables and a dip, caramelized walnuts, and a rich chocolate pâté loaf—she added, "This is my idea of a great meal—lots of appetizers followed by a good hit of chocolate. I really don't know why anybody bothers with a main course, to tell you the truth."

As the friends sampled the tasty and colourful array of food, they chatted about their gardening efforts, but it wasn't long before they returned to what had become a continuing theme. Doug wanted to hear more from Todd about his experience as an executor although, he said, "I don't have quite the same personal interest as I did when we spoke two months ago."

"Why's that?" asked Todd.

"I was going to act as executor of my mother's will, but now that she's decided to go back to Quebec and move in with her sister it could be a lot trickier with the two of us living in different jurisdictions. Apparently, Quebec's laws are quite different from the rest of Canada's—the old Napoleonic Code, and all that. She's decided to name a corporate executor with an office in Sherbrooke, someone my aunt Isobel is also planning to use.

One of the deciding factors is that she wants to rent out her house here rather than selling it, so when she dies, she'll likely have assets in both Quebec and Alberta. That would make things quite a bit trickier, apparently."

"Why wouldn't she sell her house here?" asked Fiona. "Or am I being way too nosy?"

"Not at all," said Doug. "My mom's always been a prudent sort of person. I think she wants to leave herself an escape hatch. If things don't work out with her sister, she probably figures she won't have burnt all her bridges here. Even if she stays in Quebec for the rest of her life, she seems to like the idea of receiving a monthly rent cheque. I pointed out to her that she could sell the house, invest the proceeds in an annuity, and still get a guaranteed monthly cheque but she doesn't see it that way. And, of course, I'll have the pleasure of acting as her 'Johnny on the Spot' rental agent. I should probably take a crash course on plumbing—I've always been hopeless at that sort of stuff."

"Sounds like you still got the best end of the stick, compared to being an executor," said Todd.

"Here, let me recharge everyone's glasses and you can fill us in," said Gerald.

⋘◉⋙

Sheila lobbed the first question at Todd. "How did you even know where to start?" she asked. "I imagine it's like being dropped into someone else's financial shoes and you've got to quickly put them on and start walking."

"That's a neat way of putting it, Sheila, and it does kind of describe the job. Scott's lawyer was really good at laying out all the steps I had to take and was a big help in anticipating what I might need. For example, he advised me to get at least 10 originals of the death certificate. It seems like everyone you write to needs one and a copy just doesn't cut it."

"One thing I've never been really clear on," said Fiona, "is what the word 'executor' actually means. I think a lot of people get 'executor' and 'executioner' mixed up in their minds—they both sound more than a little ominous."

"I've learned that the modern term is 'personal representative,' which covers two separate roles—executor and trustee. An executor *executes* a will by carrying out its terms, usually within the first year after death," replied Todd. "The executor might personally think that directing 90% of the estate to the Home for Wayward Cats is a ridiculous idea but if that's what the will says then he's got to do it. The only real discretion comes when the executor is also acting as trustee."

"Is that what you are, too?" asked Fiona.

"Yes—and that's probably the most challenging part of the job Scott left me with. Under the terms of Scott's will, the bulk of his estate is held in trust for his two boys. So I am the trustee of those funds until the youngest turns 21. In the meantime, I have to ensure that Denise receives sufficient and regular payments for their support. I also have to decide on what is in the boys' best interests if they want extra money to do something."

"Like travelling to Europe?" asked Sheila.

"Yes, I suppose so, or buying a Jeep with roll bars when they're 18," said Todd wryly. "I guess I'm going to have to ask myself over and over, 'Now if Scott were still around, would he want his boys to do this?' It's quite a responsibility for someone with no experience of kids."

"Except for being one," said Nori, giving Todd's arm an affectionate squeeze. "Actually, I've been really impressed with the way Todd has handled this whole deal. It certainly was very time consuming at the beginning."

"How so?" asked Fiona.

"Right off the bat, I had to make all the funeral and cremation arrangements. It's kind of surreal being taken into this big room full of caskets and urns and asked to pick out something appropriate. You can see why some people end up spending huge amounts on elaborate caskets and so on—somehow, it seems disrespectful, or something, to think about economizing at a time like that. Fortunately, Scott's will made it quite clear that he wanted the simplest arrangements possible so I didn't have to agonize too much over that issue."

"I've always thought that being a funeral director must be a very difficult job," said Vanessa. "Imagine always having to strike a balance between being reverent, on the one hand, and business-like, on the other."

"There was one moment when I thought I was going to lose it," said Todd. "As executor, I had to sign a form authorizing Scott's cremation. The funeral director looked me squarely in the eye and said, 'I am obliged to inform you, sir, that cremation is an irreversible process.' It was a moment right out of 'Monty Python'!"

"You can laugh about it, now," said Nori, "but that whole experience was pretty hard on you at the time."

"I certainly feel like I'm a different person now than I was a few months ago before all this happened. I've always been pretty casual about paying bills and dealing with bureaucracy in general. Suddenly, I'm on the phone for hours on end, cancelling Scott's lease on his apartment, dealing with cable, credit cards, subscriptions, health insurance coverage—you name it. And since I had to redirect his mail to my address, every time the letter carrier comes by, there's something new to deal with. Nothing big—a renewal request from his health club, a couple of requests for charitable donations, or a statement from his broker, but they all need to be looked at. Some of the stuff you can just ignore, but a lot of it requires action. I'm beginning to feel I've paid off my debt to Scott for all those times he cleaned out the hamster's cage in our Grade One classroom so I wouldn't have to."

"What about the tax implications?" asked Gerald. "I mean of the estate, not the hamster's cage."

"They're both full of you-know-what, in my opinion!" said Todd with a smile. "I'm hoping I can just get all the information together and dump it on an accountant—what do I know about tax laws? But what's even more terrifying than the tax stuff is that I'm responsible for how the estate is invested. Scott's will gave me fairly broad investment powers. That's pretty scary when his two boys depend on me to not goof things up. Can't you just imagine me saying, 'Your dad did leave a bunch of money for your university education but all that's left might pay for a couple of correspondence courses in TV repair'? I've pretty much decided to put the funds in a managed account and let a professional worry about it."

"Yes, I can see that would be a concern," said Gerald. "On the one hand, you'd want to be aggressive enough to get significant capital appreciation, but on the other, you wouldn't want to be taking any unnecessary risks."

"Are there sizeable funds involved?" asked Doug.

"Pretty big bucks as far as I'm concerned," said Todd. "Scott had a half million dollar life insurance policy but then there was an additional $250,000 payable in the event of accidental death. That's on top of his savings and RRSP investments, and so on. By the time those boys of his are grown up, there should be quite a substantial inheritance coming their way."

"So you'll be involved in this estate for years—until the youngest boy is 21. Is that right?" asked Fiona. "I know you feel you're helping out a friend but shouldn't you get compensated for all the time it's taking you? And nobody had better say that's a Scottish question!"

"Funny you should bring that up," said Nori. "Todd and I were discussing that very subject over dinner last night."

"I don't feel right in charging the estate for my time…" said Todd.

"And yet we've had to hire extra help in the store because Todd's been so busy with Scott's affairs," Nori added.

"Are there any guidelines?" asked Fiona.

"Yes, apparently every province has guidelines covering fees that an executor may charge. I think we've decided that I won't charge the full amount but instead we'll figure out what the extra help at the store has cost us and put in for that amount. I still feel a bit weird doing it but I guess that Scott wouldn't have wanted us to be out of pocket in taking care of his affairs."

"That sounds like the perfect solution," said Vanessa approvingly. "Now, what's the feeling on coffee? Shall I serve it inside or are we brave enough to stay outside now that the sun's gone down? It's not exactly warm, but that's Calgary for you."

"Oh, please can we stay outside?" said Fiona. "This is the first half-decent night we've had in a while. I *do* like our summers here but I think we probably pay for them the rest of the year."

"It's like that old joke," said Doug. "Calgary's weather is ten months of winter and two months of bad sledding. But I agree with Fiona. Our summers *are* great here. I'm sure my mom has forgotten how humid the weather can be in Quebec—it will probably come as a nasty shock to her."

"Pretty gutsy move on her part, you have to admit," said Nori, reaching for a sliver of chocolate pâté that was left on the serving plate. "Most older people wouldn't have the nerve to uproot themselves and make a completely fresh start."

"That's my mom," said Doug. "She's always been very independent. She was the one who brought up the business of naming a corporate executor in Quebec."

"Will she re-do her will here or wait until she gets to Quebec?" asked Nori.

"I think the plan is to wait and get a new one prepared by a lawyer who practises wills and estate law in her new place of residence. It doesn't make much sense to get it reviewed here before she goes," Doug replied.

"Isn't it kind of expensive to appoint a corporate executor?" Nori asked. "Somehow I thought only millionaires would do that. It would never have occurred to an average guy like Scott, right?"

"But Nori, the funny thing is that with Scott's life insurance, his estate is pretty close to a million bucks," said Todd. "I'm sure that a professional executor would be overkill for a lot of people but it would depend on the circumstances. As for the expense, Scott's lawyer explained that the fee an executor can charge is the same regardless of whether the work is done by someone like me or a trust company. That's actually pretty scary, when you think about it!"

"I'm sure you're doing a top-notch job," said Vanessa. "And you've got something none of those professionals have."

"What's that?" asked Todd.

"Memories of a long and wonderful friendship and a special feeling of attachment to those two boys he left behind."

"Yes," said Doug. "You've been a real friend in need—we're all impressed."

"Hey, next thing you know, we'll be crying in our beer, or our coffee, or whatever the hell it is we're drinking," said Todd gruffly. "Let's talk about something else. Where's our next get-together going to be?"

"I'm glad you brought that up," said Sheila, quickly responding to Todd's need to turn the spotlight away from his emotions. "Do you think we're up to a field trip?"

Seeing she had the others' interest, she continued. "We were scheduled to get together around the third week in July but that coincides with Fiona's walking trip in Tuscany. If we moved it up to the second week, that would put us in the middle of the Stampede. My folks won't be using their place in the country so we could all head out of town and have a chili cook-up or something equally appropriate—you know, pretend we're all cowboys out on the range. I could even line up a few gentle horses from the local stable if you fancy a trail ride."

"It *does* sound like fun," said Fiona, "and I really appreciate you working around my dates. I'd hate to miss our wind-up meeting—count me in."

"Is that okay with everyone?" asked Sheila. "That's great, then. So y'all make sure you polish up your spurs and buckle up your chaps and we'll see you in July!"

Estate

ADMINISTRATION— THE BIGGER PICTURE

At the Victoria Day celebration, our friends in the Elderberry Gate Dinner Club pick up on Todd's tale of being an executor—a responsibility placed suddenly on his shoulders upon the accidental death of his friend in January.

As Todd is experiencing, it is not uncommon for an estate to take several months, even years, to wrap up. As the saying goes, "It all depends!" Every estate is different, so, as mentioned in the January commentary, a person learning that he or she is named as an executor should seek out some good, solid professional help as soon as possible.

WHAT MAKES ONE ESTATE DIFFERENT FROM THE NEXT?

Even though each estate is a unique entity and will invariably pose unique challenges to its executor, there are some fundamental questions that arise in most estates:

- Is probate of the deceased's will required?

- Are there significant tax issues to be decided, or tax returns from previous years that need to be prepared?

- Are the gifts or distributions under the will to be made to the beneficiaries "outright," or do trusts need to be set up to hold some distributions for a number of years?

- Will the executor be paid compensation for his or her work, and if so, how much, and how and when does this payment occur?

Probate—What Is It Anyway?

In recent years there's been a lot of discussion about "avoiding probate," which has had the effect of making an already mysterious matter even murkier.

Probate is really not a difficult concept. The first thing to know is that when a person dies, in most cases, a document is found that everyone believes in good faith to be the deceased's "last will." Fortunately, the law agrees that it is perfectly fine, in such a situation, for the executor named in that document to proceed to take charge and start to act as the executor— finding and securing all the assets, dealing with debts and determining the taxes owing, reviewing the will and beginning to think about making distributions to the named beneficiaries.

The carrying out of all of these duties could quite merrily go along, right up to the final distribution, except for one little point—how to transfer the assets from the deceased's name to the executor's name, and then to the beneficiaries' names?

While the named executor and beneficiaries in this purported last will may agree among themselves that this is indeed the deceased person's last will, an outside party takes a risk if it agrees to simply transfer the deceased's assets to someone standing there with a piece of paper that is supposed to be the deceased's last will.

If that outside party—say, a bank—agrees to transfer the deceased's bank account to the alleged executor on the basis of that piece of paper, the bank takes the risk that the next day, a different person could appear at its doorstep, with a different piece of paper, stating that this piece of paper is the deceased's last will and that *he* is the duly appointed executor.

The law provides a solution to these outside parties, which include all kinds of financial service companies and land title registries, and that solution is called "probate." By completing certain forms and swearing to the truth of certain vital pieces of information, an executor named in a will can receive from the court a grant of probate. A grant of probate, or "probated will," simply is an official court order that this is in fact the last will and that everyone dealing with the estate can rely on what it says.

Because the courts are acting only on the evidence put before them, from time to time a probated will turns out to not be the last will. While this can lead to litigation and general angst among the beneficiaries who received assets and those who should have received the assets, this subsequent event does not affect those outside parties who gave the deceased's assets to the executor on the basis of the grant of probate. They did what they were supposed to do and so are not responsible to anyone who comes along later with a different will.

Why avoid probate?

Discussions about avoiding probate are often made in reference to the filing fee (really a tax in some provinces, due to the high rates) charged by the court to issue the grant of probate. If a person is concerned about the amount of the probate fee that his or her estate will be charged some day, the issue should be raised during the estate planning process. After death, if an outside party demands a grant of probate before it will give the executor the deceased's assets, there is little that can be done other than to get the will probated!

Taxes

Unless an executor is ready to pay the deceased's outstanding taxes out of his or her own pocket, the executor should make getting a grip on the tax situation a matter of first priority.

Taxing statutes in Canada, whether dealing with income tax or goods and services tax, or any other tax, are crystal clear on one point: An executor who distributes assets from an estate that still owes taxes is in trouble i.e., he or she will be held personally responsible for the payment of those taxes.

Although some estates have very simple tax issues to address (for example, only the filing of the final tax return and a request for a "clearance certificate"), other estates are much more complicated. Some people die being in arrears in taxes or will have been directors or shareholders in companies that never got around to filing returns—the executor must then do so. Some other estates will take a long time to be wound up, so in addition to the last tax return while the deceased was alive, there will be ongoing estate returns declaring the income earned by the estate, for example, interest, capital gains, or dividend income.

A complete review of the potential tax issues in estates is far beyond the scope of this discussion. The point to be made here is that a smart executor will retain a good accountant to review the deceased's affairs to make sure that all the tax items are addressed. As is the case with every profession, some accountants have particular interest and experience in estate tax matters; if you are an executor, find one of these specialists—ideally through your network of trusted people—to protect your interests.

Gifts from the Estate—Now or Later?

An important question for an executor is whether the distributions out of the estate are (1) to be made ASAP to the beneficiaries, to be fully handed over to those people to do with as they like, or (2) to be held in trust for the beneficiaries for a while.

Many wills contain both types of gifts. For example, a will may give an assortment of personal items (such as jewellery) to certain named people, a few gifts of cash to some charities, and then direct that the rest is to be set aside in a trust for all the deceased person's grandchildren. In this example, the personal items and the charitable bequests are called outright gifts and the trusts set up for the grandchildren are called—you guessed it!—gifts held in trust.

As Todd discovered, gifts to be held in trust require more time and attention than merely sending out cheques or necklaces. Trusts set up under the terms of a will also usually require the executor to exercise some judgement on a number of points, such as how to invest the trust funds. The scope of the executor's discretion will be determined by the powers set out in the will—some wills give the executors a lot of discretion, others permit the executors to act in a fairly circumscribed way.

The advising lawyer will offer advice on such matters as the initial set up of trusts described in the will, how the trusts should be managed in the future, how the funds can be invested, and the procedure for making distributions to the beneficiaries.

This guidance may be supplemented by other advice from, say, accountants and investment advisers. However, it is important that the executor remember that he or she is ultimately responsible for the decisions. It may be worthwhile to obtain second or even third opinions on the really big issues, in order for the executor to finally make a fully informed and independent decision. An executor should never feel that advice from even the most seasoned professional is necessarily the best decision for the estate.

Executor Compensation

Getting paid for being an executor feels awkward to some people. Sure, there are professional executors (more on them later), but if you are acting as the executor for a friend or a relative, you may think that you aren't entitled to claim a fee.

Legally speaking, you are in fact entitled to executor's compensation, and you should give some thought as to whether it may make sense to be paid for your work. This is easier if the will states an amount that the executor is to receive, either by giving the executor a larger gift than the other beneficiaries, or by directing payment of an executor's fee. Another possibility is that the will can set out a *method* whereby the executor's compensation should be calculated; again, this will reassure the executor that the deceased wanted the executor to be paid for the time and effort of being the executor. However, most wills for some reason do not include a direction that the executor be paid.

Even if the will makes no mention of executor compensation, provincial legislation, supported by the court's rules and regulations in each province, direct that an executor is *entitled* to be paid, and generally also gives guidelines on the amount. Some of these provisions use fairly vague wording, referring to notions such as "fair and reasonable compensation."

Sometimes there are also relevant factors set out in the provincial legislation or court's rules, and over the years, courts have frequently been asked to consider what should be paid to executors in particular estates. Some of these relevant factors are

- the gross value of the estate;
- the complexity of the work involved and whether any difficult questions were raised;
- the amount of skill, labour, and specialized knowledge required; and
- time expended.

There is no end of advice to be had out there, and in the final analysis, an executor may simply do as Todd did—take a sufficient fee to approximately cover his lost income from the business he runs. When there is more than one executor, the total amount of the fee is the same—after all, the work on an estate is the same, regardless of how many people divide the tasks. It is then up to the executors to figure out how this fee will be shared among them—if they can't agree on that, the court would have to decide.

In summary, on the amount of an executors fee, note that disbursements, such as reasonable travel expenses from the executor's home to where the estate work needs to be done, are always reimbursed to the executor, and are not really in the same category as a fee for the time and effort expended.

If the will sets out a specific fee for the executor, then obviously there is no decision that needs to be made on the amount to be paid to the executor. In all other cases, once an executor has looked at (or received advice about) the appropriate range of compensation for the estate at hand, a decision is made as to what he or she will actually request. The key word here is "request," because an executor cannot unilaterally decide what to be paid—it must be agreed to by all the beneficiaries or else approved by a court. Only after this approval has occurred can the executor be paid.

Usually the payment of the executor's fee is one of the last things to happen in an estate administration but again, with the agreement of all the beneficiaries or court approval, an executor can be authorized to receive some of the executor's fee before all the work is done.

CORPORATE EXECUTORS

Much of the May dinner conversation revolved around the work Todd had been doing as his friend's executor and the decision of Doug's mother to appoint a trust company as her executor instead of her son.

Why a Corporate Executor?

Geography is one of the most common reasons why people think about corporate executors. Another factor is that potential executors within the family—even those located nearby—do not have the time, skill, interest, or inclination. As discussed above and in the January commentary, the role of an executor is diverse, challenging, time-consuming, potentially risky, and often subject to criticism from beneficiaries. An executor should therefore be financially astute, highly organized, good with small details and deadlines but also able to grasp the big picture, and empathetic with beneficiaries. If you have trouble finding someone to agree to being your executor, don't take it personally!

Frankly, some estates are best administered by a corporate executor. For one thing, a corporate executor, since it is a corporate entity (trust company) will always have qualified personnel to administer estates. In contrast, a human being appointed as an executor may die before the person signing the will dies, or worse, die before finishing the estate administration.

You should be thinking of a corporate executor if your estate has any of these features:

- A fairly significant value (likely net assets over $500,000)
- An expectation of conflict among the beneficiaries
- Beneficiaries with special needs
- Complicated assets such as an active business which was run almost exclusively by the person signing the will
- One or more trusts set up in the will
- A complicated estate plan requiring the implementation of a number of tax-minimizing strategies

Some Typical Concerns

People often have some concerns about appointing a corporate executor.

The first concern may be that there will be a significant cost involved. However, as discussed above, even an individual named as an executor is entitled to a fee and, for the time and effort involved, should likely accept one! Expecting that an individual you name will *not* take a fee is likely both naïve and unfair. Either you are expecting the person to work for a year—on and off, at least—for "free," or you accept that he or she will be paid.

As well, consider the fact that an individual is often more inclined (and wisely so) to retain professional advisers, such as lawyers and accountants. A trust company typically has significant in-house expertise to handle the preparation of the probate application and tax returns, subject to review by outside advisers.

Furthermore, even when a trust company retains lawyers and accountants, the objective professionals working for the trust company tend to be assertive in negotiating exactly what the professionals are to do and not do, and exactly what the related charges will be for these services.

Some trust companies taking on corporate executor appointments discuss and commit to the exact manner in which the fee will be calculated when the time comes, giving the individual appointing the company a high degree of certainty as to what the corporate trustee will be paid for its work. Of course, this is paid only after the person dies and the work is done, or substantially completed, as outlined above.

Another concern is the level of responsiveness available from a corporate trustee. What if the nice person you deal with is no longer working for the company when you die? The best answer to this is that the bar has been raised for service standards in all areas of commerce—it's highly competitive out there! The combination of a more discerning and demanding public, together with increased competition in all fields, including trust services, means that high standards are being set and maintained.

Ideally, no matter when you make your will, you will have many years left to enjoy life, and if you've appointed a trust company, you will have the chance to keep in touch with the trust company for will reviews, regular discussions, and information sessions. If the service standards are maintained over the years, these meetings provide you with a good idea as to what your executor and beneficiaries can expect.

THE *Menu*

❧❦❧

Smoked salmon corn cakes with lemon crème fraîche

*Savoury cheesecake with roasted red pepper
and almond pesto*

Caramelized onion and mushroom squares with feta cheese

Fresh market vegetables with lentil, lime, and sunflower dip

Spicy caramelized pecans and walnuts

Chocolate pâté with sweet noodle wafers

❧❦❧

Smoked salmon corn cakes with lemon crème fraîche

Be aware that you will need to prepare the lemon crème fraîche at least three days before serving.

½ cup	cornmeal, plus extra, for coating	125 mL
1¼ cups	all-purpose flour	300 mL
1 tsp.	baking soda	5 mL
1 tsp.	salt	5 mL
¼ tsp.	freshly ground black pepper	1 mL
½ cup	frozen corn	125 mL
½	red pepper, finely diced	½
6 ounces	smoked salmon (lox style, not BBQ), chopped	170 g
4 ounces	cream cheese, softened	125 g
2 tbsp.	chopped, fresh chives	25 mL
½ cup	heavy cream (35% M.F.)	125 mL
½ cup	milk	125 mL
1 tbsp.	fresh lemon juice	15 mL
4	eggs, lightly beaten	4
2	shallots, finely diced	2
½ tsp.	sambal oelek (see page 108)	2 mL
	Zest of ½ lemon	
	Canola oil and butter for frying	

1. In a medium-sized bowl, combine the dry ingredients.

2. In a large bowl, combine all the remaining ingredients and stir to blend.

3. Add the dry ingredients to the wet ingredients and stir until just blended. Do not over-mix.

4. Heat 1 teaspoon (5 mL) of canola oil and 1 teaspoon (5 mL) of butter in a skillet, over medium-high heat, until sizzling. Form batter into 2-inch (10 cm) rounds, about ½-inch (1 cm) thick. Coat them lightly with the extra cornmeal. Fry the cakes until golden brown and crisp. Cool slightly. (If you are making the corn cakes in advance, allow them to cool, wrap well, refrigerate for no more than 2 days, then reheat on a baking sheet, in a 375°F (190°C) oven for about 10 minutes.)

Lemon crème fraîche

1 cup	heavy cream, (35% M.F.)	250 mL
2 tbsp.	buttermilk	25 mL
	Zest of 1 lemon	

1. Pour the cream and buttermilk into a glass jar with an airtight lid. Stir to blend, cover, and store at room temperature for 36 hours. Refrigerate for a minimum of 24 hours. The crème fraîche should now be as thick as yogurt.

2. Add the lemon zest to the crème fraîche and stir to blend.

Savoury cheesecake with roasted red pepper and almond pesto

This rich appetizer may be eaten in very thin wedges, or used as a spread, with crackers or pita chips (see page 25).

Crust

1 package	Wheat Thins	1 pkg.
¼ cup	cold butter, cut into ½-inch (1 cm) cubes	50 mL
¼ cup	grated fresh Parmesan cheese	50 mL
½ tsp.	dried oregano	2 mL
¼ tsp.	black pepper	1 mL

1. Heat oven to 350ºF (180ºC).

2. In a food processor, process the Wheat Thins to fine crumbs.

3. Add the butter, Parmesan cheese, dried oregano, and pepper. Pulse until the mixture holds together when pinched between a thumb and finger.

4. Press the mixture into the bottom and sides of a 10-inch (25 cm) springform pan. Bake until golden brown, approximately 15 minutes. Remove from the oven. It is not necessary to cool the crust at this point.

Filling

1½ lb.	cream cheese	750 g
1 tsp.	sugar	5 mL
1 tbsp.	flour	15 mL
½ cup	heavy cream (35% M.F.)	125 mL
3	eggs	3
½ tsp.	salt	2 mL
¼ tsp.	white pepper	1 mL
1 tbsp.	coriander chutney	
	(see page 70)	15 mL
½	red pepper, finely diced	½

1. Heat oven to 425°F (225°C).

2. Beat the cream cheese with an electric mixer until light and soft. Add the sugar, flour, and cream and beat for 1 minute. Scrape down the sides and bottom of the bowl. Add the eggs one at a time, beating for 1 minute after each addition—don't forget to keep scraping down the bowl! Add the salt, white pepper, coriander chutney, and diced red pepper. Mix well. Taste the cream cheese mixture. If it doesn't taste good to you now, it won't after it's cooked! Adjust seasonings. If you find it a bit flat, add a squeeze of fresh lime or a bit of sambal oelek. Pour the mixture into the prepared shell.

3. Bake at 425°F (220°C) for 10 minutes, then reduce the oven temperature to 250°F (120°C), and bake an additional 35 minutes. Turn off the oven, open the oven door, and allow the cake to cool for 1 hour before removing it from the oven. Cool the cake to room temperature, then refrigerate it for at least 3 hours, or overnight.

4. Spread a ⅛-inch (3 mm) layer of roasted red pepper and almond pesto over the entire surface of the cheesecake. Remove it from the spring-form pan and place it on a cake stand or plate.

Roasted red pepper and almond pesto

2 cloves	garlic	2 cloves
1½ cup	unblanched, sliced almonds	300 mL
1	dried chili, rehydrated by steeping for 15 minutes in very hot water	1
3	roasted red peppers*	3
2 tbsp.	coarsely chopped, fresh coriander	25 mL
2 tbsp.	red wine vinegar	25 mL
2 tbsp.	extra virgin olive oil	25 mL
2	green onions, trimmed and coarsely chopped	2
	Salt and freshly ground pepper	

* To roast peppers, hold them over an open flame or put them in a very hot oven until the skin is black on all sides. Put them in a plastic bag or covered container for 15 minutes, to steam. Peel and seed the peppers in cool water, then pat them dry, and coat them well with olive oil. Store them in the refrigerator for up to 5 days, or in the freezer for up to 2 months.

1. Put garlic, almonds, and chili in the bowl of a food processor and process to a fine crumb.

2. Add the remaining ingredients, except salt and pepper, and process until evenly mixed but still a bit coarse in texture, like mincemeat. Season with salt and freshly ground pepper, to taste.

Carmelized onion and mushroom squares with feta cheese

This delicious and versatile tart may be cut into large wedges and served hot as the centrepiece of a brunch menu; cut into small squares and served warm or at room temperature as an appetizer; or cut into larger pieces and served in place of bread or rolls with dinner. Unlike most yeast breads, it can be made one day in advance and refrigerated, or several days in advance and frozen. In either case, reheat it in the oven, not in the microwave.

Crust

½ tsp.	sugar	2 mL
1 tbsp.	dry yeast	15 mL
1 cup	warm water	250 mL
2 tsp.	salt	10 mL
1	egg, lightly beaten	1
2½ to 3 cups	all-purpose flour	625 to 750 mL
2 tbsp.	soft butter	25 mL

1. In the bowl of a stand mixer, dissolve the sugar and yeast in the warm water.

2. When the yeast is slightly bubbly, add the salt and egg. Using the dough hook, mix in the flour, ½ cup (125 mL) at a time. After having added the first 2 cups (500 mL), mix in the butter. Add more flour until the dough is soft and sticky, but smooth. The dough on the hook and the dough in the bowl are still attached by long and very elastic strands when you raise the hook from the bowl. Cover with plastic wrap and allow to rise until doubled in volume, approximately 1½ hours.

Filling

¼ cup	butter	50 mL
2	large onions, sliced lengthwise, ⅛-inch (3 mm) thick	2
1 lb.	mushrooms, thinly sliced	500 g
1 clove	garlic, minced	1 clove
3	eggs	3
¾ cup	heavy cream (35% M.F.)	175 mL
1 tbsp.	fresh herbs, such as basil, oregano, parsley, chervil, or chives	15 mL
2 dashes	Tabasco sauce	2 dashes
1 dash	Worcestershire sauce	1 dash
	Zest of ½ lemon	
	Salt and pepper	
6 ounces	feta cheese, coarsely crumbled	170g

1. Melt half the butter in a skillet over medium high heat.

2. Add the onions. Cook them until just beginning to brown. Decrease the temperature and cook, stirring frequently, until they are soft and uniformly caramel coloured, approximately 30 minutes. Cool slightly.

3. In a separate skillet, over high heat, melt the remaining butter and add the mushrooms. Stirring frequently, cook them until uniformly brown, reducing heat as needed. Add the garlic and continue to cook for 1 minute. Cool slightly.

4. In a large mixing bowl, whisk together all the remaining ingredients, *except* the feta. Stir in the caramelized onions, mushrooms, and feta.

To Assemble

1. Heat the oven to 375°F (190ºC).

2. Spread the dough onto an oiled 11 x 17 (27 x 42 cm) inch baking sheet.

3. Cover the dough evenly with filling.

4. Bake for approximately 30 minutes, until golden brown and set.

Fresh market vegetables with lentil, lime, and sunflower dip

Fresh Vegetable Crudités

When choosing vegetables for use as crudités, select only the freshest, preferably seasonal, vegetables. In Canada, where most of our fresh vegetables are imported year round, it's best to simply choose whatever appears freshest and most abundant.

Lentil, Lime, and Sunflower Dip

If you are able to find organically grown sunflowers, chop up some of the petals and fold them into this dip to add a bit of colour and textural interest.

½ cup	dried red lentils	125 mL
	Salt	
2 cloves	garlic, minced	2 cloves
½ cup	sunflower seeds, roasted and salted	125 mL
	Juice and zest of 1 lime	
2 tbsp.	coarsely chopped chives	25 mL

2 tbsp.	coarsely chopped basil	25 mL
1 tbsp.	mayonnaise	15 mL
	Tabasco sauce	
	Salt and freshly ground black pepper	

1. Wash the lentils and pick them over for stones. Bring 4 cups (1 L) of cold water to a boil. Add 1 teaspoon (5 ml) of salt and the lentils. Simmer, uncovered until tender, about 20 minutes. Drain and cool.

2. Put the garlic and sunflower seeds in the bowl of a food processor. Process to a fine crumb.

3. Add the cooked lentils, lime zest and juice, chives, and basil. Process to a coarse paste.

4. Add the mayonnaise and a dash of Tabasco sauce, and pulse to blend. Season with salt and pepper. Refrigerate for at least 2 hours to allow the flavours to come together.

Spicy caramelized pecans and walnuts

1 tbsp.	olive oil	15 mL
½ tsp.	cinnamon	2 mL
½ tsp.	curry powder	2 mL
½ tsp.	ground ginger	2 mL
⅛ tsp.	cayenne (or more, if you like it hot)	0.5 mL
2 tbsp.	sugar	25 mL
2 tbsp.	honey	25 mL
¾ cup	walnut halves	175 mL
¾ cup	pecan halves	175 mL
	Salt	

1. In a large skillet, heat the olive oil, cinnamon, curry powder, ginger, cayenne, sugar, and honey over medium-high heat until the sugar is dissolved, about 5 minutes.

2. Add the nuts. Reduce the heat and cook, stirring, for about 25 minutes, until the candy is no longer sticky when cool. (To test, put one nut on a plate, in the freezer. When it's cool, it should be crisp, not chewy.)

3. Spread the nuts on a lightly oiled baking sheet, and sprinkle them with salt. Separate the nuts with a spoon while they are cooling. When completely cool, store in an airtight container.

Chocolate pâté with sweet noodle wafers

Chocolate pâté*

Dark, rich, and slightly boozy, this chocolate pâté is certain to garner much extravagant praise from your chocolate-loving guests. It may be served sliced, with a fresh berry or custard sauce, or as a spread, accompanied by butter cookies, crisp meringues, pretzels, or sweet noodle wafers.

1 lb.	dark chocolate (the better the chocolate, the better the pâté)	500 g
1 cup	heavy cream (35% M.F.)	250 mL
2 ounces	butter	50 g
4	egg yolks	4

---

*Adapted from Alan Richman, "Diets be Damned! Bring on Dessert!" *Food and Wine*, October 1987, 156.

| ¾ cup | icing sugar | 175 mL |
| ¼ cup | brandy or dark rum | 50 mL |

1. Line a loaf pan with plastic wrap.

2. In a heavy-bottomed saucepan, over low to medium heat, melt the chocolate, cream, and butter until smooth. Remove from heat.

3. Whisk in the egg yolks, one at a time until well blended. Whisk in the sugar and liquor. Pour the mixture into the loaf pan and refrigerate for at least 6 hours. Turn the pâté onto a cake plate, dust with cocoa, and decorate with fresh or crystallized flowers. Surround with sweet noodle wafers.

Sweet noodle wafers

Be sure to use fresh oil to fry these wafers. They will take on any lingering flavour from used or old oil.

	Peanut oil, for frying	
20	won ton or gyoza wrappers, sliced in half, diagonally	20
	Icing sugar	

1. In a large skillet, heat ½ inch (1 cm) of peanut oil over medium-high heat. To test, drop one drop of water into the hot oil—if it sputters noisily, it's ready.

2. Drop in the won ton wrappers, one at a time (a large skillet will hold five or six at once). When they're golden on one side, flip each one and fry until uniformly golden. Do not allow them to turn brown. If

you find that they are browning too quickly, reduce the burner temperature.

3. Put them on a newspaper covered with paper towels. Allow them to cool. Dust both sides with icing sugar shaken from a fine sieve.

Advance Preparation

At least three days before the party, prepare the crème fraîche.

Two days before the party:
Prepare the roasted red pepper pesto and the pita chips.

The day before the party:
Make the lentil, lime, and sunflower dip, the caramelized walnuts and pecans, the savoury cheesecake, and the chocolate pâté.

The day of the party:
Make the smoked salmon corn cakes, the caramelized onion and mushroom squares, and the sweet noodle wafers. Prepare the vegetable crudités.

Shorly before the guests arrive:

Place on serving plates anything that is to be served cold. Cover well with plastic wrap until ready to serve. Don't prepare the hot items until at least a few guests have arrived, and even then, don't do too many at once.

Home
ON THE RANGE

"Vanessa, Fiona, is that everything?" asked Gerald, preparing to slam the trunk shut on the Porters' Audi. "I can't imagine there could possibly be anything more that we need—this is a day's outing to a cabin, you know, not a year-long wilderness expedition!"

As they followed Highway 8 out of the city, the sterile gridwork of urban sprawl soon gave way to undulating fields, brilliantly green with new hay. Beyond the golden bands of last year's stubble and the glittering flashes of prairie sloughs stood the mountains, calm and austere in the early morning light. A faint heat haze shimmered on the road before them, promising a welcome change from the cool wet days of early July.

Before long, they turned south, diligently following Doug's SUV and travelling deeper into the rolling foothills of the Rockies' eastern flank. Open fields gave way to more craggy ranchland. Livestock grazed unconcerned as the two vehicles rumbled noisily over cattle grids and gravel roads.

"Has this cabin been in Sheila's family for a while?" asked Fiona.

"I think so," Vanessa replied. "Haven't you ever heard those wonderful stories about the big branding parties they used to hold? Sheila said her mother had to bake for weeks to come up with all the fruit pies they needed for helpers and friends. Her dad would build a BBQ pit and they'd roast hips of beef all day in readiness for the party at night. Of course, the whole ranching operation got to be more than they could handle and they sold it a number of years ago, just keeping the main house and a few acres around it as a weekend place. According to Sheila, they'd have made a fortune if they'd hung on to it for a few more years. Hindsight is golden, as they say."

"Tell me about it," said Fiona. "I got a phone call the other day from an old friend and neighbour of ours. She wanted to visit Dad in the nursing home. She asked me whether I'd heard that our old house had been sold again—seems like the guy who bought it from Dad only a couple of years ago flipped it and made a cool $50,000 on the deal."

"That's a booming economy for you," said Gerald. "Quite a contrast from the '80s when people were walking away from their mortgages. Did you tell your dad or did you decide to spare him the news?"

"Oh, I told him all right, but he just smiled and said, 'That's nice, dear. Make sure you don't spend it all at once.' I'm afraid he's slipping fast. The other day he went for a walk around the ward and the nurses found him curled up having a nap in some lady's bed—fortunately, she wasn't there at the time! I was so embarrassed for him but apparently, it happens quite often. I guess the rooms look pretty much alike so it's quite common for the patients to play musical beds!"

"Gosh, we have so much to look forward to, don't we?" said Vanessa, peering through the car window at a hawk hovering motionless aloft. "Although there could be some positives, I suppose. Maybe Gerald in his dotage will forget he likes Wagner!"

"Not a chance," said Gerald laughing. "I've stipulated in my personal directive that I want someone to come in and play my Ring Cycle CDs to me every Friday afternoon whether I'm *compos mentis* or not!"

"That reminds me," said Vanessa. "Did you ever get your personal directive business sorted out, Fiona?"

"Yes, it's quite a weight off my mind, especially since I'm leaving for Tuscany in less than two weeks, as you know. It was good to have that as an incentive to get all my affairs in order."

"It's funny you should say that," said Vanessa. "Going abroad often seems to have a strange effect on people. It's almost like they need to have everything taken care of before they go—you know, cancel the newspaper, clean out the refrigerator, and write the will."

"I suppose it is kind of funny. I wonder if deep in our unconscious we fear that going overseas is somehow a dangerous activity—one we might not return from alive!"

"The last time we spoke you were trying to figure out who you would name to take care of your affairs," said Vanessa. "What did you end up doing?"

"I agonized over whether I should ask my god-daughter Megan. It seemed like such an imposition, especially since she isn't really family. Her mother and I were roommates in college and while I think of Barbara like a sister, she isn't, of course. In the end, I took Megan out to lunch, just the two of us. I didn't want to put any undue pressure on her, but the whole process turned out to be a lot easier than I had imagined. As soon as I brought up the subject, she said she'd just gone through that with her mom and that she'd be honoured to do the same for me. I didn't even have to ask her!"

"That's great, Fiona! And did you get the business of naming beneficiaries taken care of as well?" asked Vanessa.

"Yep—Megan was a big help in that regard too. She was talking about having to work two jobs while doing her master's at the University of Calgary. It gave me the idea of setting up some kind of endowment fund to help young women starting off in the energy industry. Nowadays, there's no shortage of female engineering graduates, all very proficient in technical knowledge but most of them missing the necessary management skills to do well in the business arena. So I met with the Faculty of Management and we've got some scholarship plans in place. There's certainly a tax advantage in giving some of the money now, and I was able to get my old firm to match my donations while they still remember my name!"

"What a terrific idea!" said Gerald. "It sounds like a win-win situation all round."

"Yes," said Fiona. "I'm feeling really good about it and I still had the freedom to name Megan as a personal beneficiary, of course."

"You'll have to let the others know," said Vanessa. "I've got a feeling that just about everyone has got their house in order. Dinner tonight might be a time for self-congratulation—a nice way to end the dinner club year, don't you think?"

"Yep—but in the meantime, we've got cars to unpack, horses to ride, and chili to stir. Let's get at it," said Fiona as Gerald pulled up at a rustic log house. "And if I'm still in one piece by suppertime, I'll be glad to fill the others in."

⁂

By late afternoon, the residents of Elderberry Gate had returned to the cabin, tired and a little saddle sore, but otherwise in high spirits. A few hours of gentle trekking had done wonders for their appetites although, as Sheila pointed out, they never had much difficulty in that department anyway. Nori and Todd, who had gone for a walk rather than a ride, took pity on the weary group and fired up the barbecue to heat the quesadillas. Dinner was still an hour or so away but the fresh air had made them all even more ready for food than usual.

⸎

"Boy, those quesadillas hit the spot," said Doug, licking his fingers. "I've never thought of cooking them on an outdoor grill before—it sure brings out the taste of the smoked turkey."

"Just make sure you do them on medium heat," said Todd. "That way the cheese gets nicely melted before the tortillas get burned and crispy. I have to admit it was Nori who pointed out to me that our gas barbecue actually had heat settings."

⸎

Somewhat restored by their snack, the group engaged in a rousing game of horseshoes, but before long, they were back at the table on the verandah digging in to Doug and Sheila's chili.

"This chili is outstanding," said Todd. "Where did you get the recipe?"

"My brother Bill takes part in an annual chili cook-off," said Sheila. "This was the prize-winning recipe from last year."

"It's certainly a keeper," said Vanessa, "and I definitely want to know how to make these savoury scones, Fiona. They're out of this world."

"Thanks, Vanessa," Fiona replied. "I hope to come back from my trip to Italy inspired to try a lot of new things. You never know what you'll be getting from my kitchen next year."

"I'd forgotten that your trip is coming up," said Doug. "I bet you'll have a wonderful time. There isn't room for any of us in your suitcase, I suppose?"

"No," said Fiona, laughing. "I have to say I'm really looking forward to it. It will be my first real holiday in years. I just hope my dad's okay while I'm gone. There's no reason why he shouldn't be—half the time I'm visiting, I don't think he has a clue who I am. Still, I wouldn't be true to my Scottish Presbyterian roots if I didn't feel a touch of guilt. At least I've got my personal affairs in order before I leave."

"Fiona was filling us in on the way here," Vanessa said to the others. "She's done a great job. I rather suspect we've all made some advances on that front. How about I serve dessert and we can have show and tell time?"

❧❧❧

Over ice cream and cookies, Nori and Todd began to talk about the progress they'd made with their wills.

"It's too bad that it had to be the loss of my friend that finally got us going," said Todd. "It makes me think of that corny saying, 'If life serves you lemons, make lemonade.' Scott's death was a real tragedy but I like to think that something positive came out of it."

"Hear, hear," said Gerald.

"Of course, just when we thought we were all set, we've discovered we'll have to pay our lawyer one more visit in the new year."

"Why's that?" asked Fiona.

"We didn't address the issue of guardianship," said Todd.

"Of whom? You don't have any children. Ah, *I* get it," said Vanessa, jumping to her feet. "Congratulations! When's the happy date, Nori?"

"The beginning of January—I'm hoping I'll be able to make it through the Christmas rush."

"Todd! Nori!" cried Fiona. "That's wonderful! I want you to promise to put me right at the top of your list of babysitters."

"Well, I have to admit we didn't exactly plan this," said Nori. "But now that we're becoming used to the idea, we're getting quite excited."

"Quite excited!" Todd smiled indulgently. "You should see our place—it's full of baby magazines and samples of nursery wallpaper. I think it's pretty accurate to say that we're both over the moon."

"Couldn't have happened to a nicer couple," said Doug, raising his wine glass. "One thing's for sure, your life will never be the same again. Jason is giving us a bit of a ride for our money right now but I can't imagine never having had him."

"That's true," said Sheila. "I find no matter how exasperated I get with him, I only have to think back to when he was a little guy—the memory of tucking him into bed all clean and fresh from his bath makes me ready to forgive him anything."

"Anything?" said Doug in a surprised voice.

"Well, *almost* anything. I must admit that we've put one of my big fears to rest by setting up the trust fund in our wills. I'm sure Jason is going to turn out just fine in the end—it just might take him a little while longer than most to get there. At least now we can quit worrying that he'll waste his inheritance on sex, drugs, and rock 'n' roll. And even more important, we can rest assured knowing that we have valid wills instead of a bunch of worthless paper."

"Shall we take our coffee around the fire?" asked Vanessa. "The air's cooling off, but it seems a shame to go inside."

"Sure," said Doug. "I'll get a chair set up for Nori. Sheila, is there a blanket she could have?"

"Guys!" laughed Nori. "I'm pregnant, not sick. Still, thanks very much for all the attention. I guess I should lap it up and be grateful."

"Darned right," said Vanessa. "This is your time to be treated like a queen—just enjoy it!"

❧

When the group reassembled to sit around the fire, the sun had disappeared from view but the tip of the furthest peak to the west remained bathed in a clear pink light. Overhead, the sky had shaded to a deep cobalt blue and the first stars had begun to emerge.

"Too bad we have to go back to the city tonight," said Doug. "It looks like it might be a good night for the northern lights."

"Oh," cried Fiona. "Those were just amazing on those oilfield trips I used to make to the Arctic. I haven't ever seen them at this latitude."

"It's surprising how much you can see once you get away from the city," said Sheila. As if to prove her point, a faint trail of light from an orbiting satellite traced an arc over their heads.

"Looking up at the night sky makes you feel quite small, doesn't it?' said Todd.

"Yes, and very grateful to be part of a wonderful group of friends," said Fiona. "This year would have been a lot more difficult for me without the support and care from all of you."

"Same goes for me," said Todd. "But I think the person I most want to thank is Vanessa. Without her keeping us on track, I'm not sure we would ever have got our acts together. Here's to you, Vanessa, the queen of dinner parties *and* estate planning!"

"Goodness me, Todd, I'll accept the dinner party stuff with thanks but estate planning? Don't forget when we started off this year, Gerald and I didn't have wills and we'd brought the fine art of procrastination to a new level. But somehow we all seem to have muddled through and got the job done, one way or another."

"Mostly because we were embarrassed we'd have nothing to report when you enquired at the next dinner club meeting!" said Sheila.

"You're beginning to make me feel like a dragon lady," said Vanessa with a laugh. "Next year we need to take up a new cause and let someone else be the slave driver. On second thought, I think I know who's going to be running the show at Elderberry Gate next year."

"You *do?*" said Todd.

"Yes, he or she will be living at your house and will have us all ready to jump at the shake of a rattle. I'm delighted about your baby—it will be wonderful to have a new little life in our midst."

"To new life," said Gerald, raising his coffee cup, "and to good friends. May we all enjoy good health, much happiness, and long life. And if anyone would like to enjoy good music, I've got a great Wagner CD for the drive home to the city."

"Gerald, you're incorrigible," said Vanessa, shaking her head. "Thank goodness we don't have any road trips planned for this summer. How much Wagner can normal human beings be subjected to before they go right over the edge?"

"I think we're about to find out!" said Fiona. "It's probably time we should be heading back. If I don't see all of you before I leave for Italy, have a wonderful summer. Will we have a dinner club meeting in September?"

"Don't worry," said Vanessa. "It's all in hand. I'm sure by then we'll be ready for some more food for thought."

Just DO IT!

Whether it is the arrival of a baby, or months spent in the throes of sorting out a young friend's estate, for many of us, estate planning begins only when mortality pokes us like a stick. But so what? If, like the members of the Elderberry Gate Dinner Club, you can ultimately make light of the situation and begin to plan, it doesn't really matter that it was not the intellectual side of your brain that got you to the task.

Even with the intellect and the heart firmly engaged in the process, we nevertheless tend to procrastinate on estate planning. To overcome this common inertia, a plan of attack may help—a six-step plan, as a matter of fact, that looks like this:

1. First of all, set goals.

Set goals for exactly what you want to accomplish and by when (don't just say "before I die").

Ensuring your affairs are in order after you die means you need at least a good and valid will. If you lead a slightly more complicated life, you may need other planning done, like a shareholders' agreement. To cover the possibility that you will become mentally incompetent before you die, you will need the kind of power of attorney that out-lasts your ability to make financial decisions for yourself. Protecting your personal well-being if you become mentally incompetent means you need a personal directive, or whatever that document may be called in your province.

So your goals are a *will*, an *enduring power of attorney*, and a *personal directive*—and don't forget about *setting a date* to get all this done.

2. NAIL DOWN YOUR PICKS FOR EXECUTOR AND GUARDIAN.

Get over the idea that no one can raise your children like you can so therefore logic dictates you can't do a will! That's right, no one is the terrific parent that you are—but if you're not around someone will have to take on that important role ... *who*? On the choice of your executor, see the "Top 10" points in January (page 99).

3. SPEND SOME TIME CHOOSING A PROFESSIONAL TO HELP YOU OUT.

A solid recommendation from a colleague or friend is a good start. People you trust, with affairs reasonably similar to your own, can give you an unbiased description of their estate planning experience.

You may need both a lawyer and an accountant. Don't hesitate to call and ask questions before you retain them. Ask about the likely fee, the number of meetings required, when you can expect to receive draft documents, the total time from start to finish, and how long the lawyer has been practising law. In checking out a potential wills lawyer, you may even want to ask how many wills he or she drafts on a regular basis.

Also ask whether the lawyer uses "plain English" in documents. There is no reason why your will should not make complete sense to you upon a careful reading. Never sign a document that is presented to you with the comment that it is all "legalese." Ask for, and expect to receive, documents that make sense to you.

Keep in mind that it is completely reasonable to request a range in which the fee will fall. You may even be given a firm quote if it appears to the professional involved that the planning will not be overly complex.

4. STICK WITH THE PROCESS!

A real hazard is letting those draft documents sit in the same pile as home-and-school newsletters and grocery lists. Try to read them through as soon as they arrive in the mail. Most wills have four basic parts:

- The introduction and appointment of executors and trustees
- The description of how everything you own at your death is to be divided up
- A long list of the "powers" of the executors and trustees as they are doing their work
- The appointment of guardians for your minor children

Then there is the part at the end where you and the two witnesses sign.

What is the difference between an executor and a trustee? You may want to think of the executor as the sprinter, and the trustee as the marathon runner. In the year or so after death, the executor winds up the deceased's affairs, gets the legal work done, attends to taxes and so on. After that work is done, the trustee holds the assets until the will says that they are to be distributed. So, for example, if young children are beneficiaries, the trustee's work may go on for years.

The confusing part is that in the vast majority of cases, the executor and trustee are the same person or persons so it is simply a gradual change in the type of responsibilities. It is really hard to capture the necessary legal niceties about the executor's powers in an easy-to-understand way. These powers reflect both the law handed down by the courts and the law set out in provincial and federal statutes. For example, it is common to give the executor the power to make investments outside of those investments that are prescribed by law for trustees.

That may sound like a very bad idea, but it may make sense once you understand that the prescribed investments for executors in some Canadian provinces are narrow and may be more conservative than your current investment objectives. If that is true, you may see the wisdom in giving your executor the power to invest outside of those prescribed investments. As with all powers, the executor must exercise the investment power in the manner of a prudent executor and cannot use this power as a way to sidestep the overall plan that you have set out in the will. In contrast to the "powers" section, the part of the draft will covering the actual distribution of your estate should be crystal clear.

Here are some points to keep in mind. First, the will is drafted on the basis that the lawyer doesn't know when you will die so it is essential to cover several different scenarios. The best way to do that is to state that X will occur if your spouse survives you. *But*, if your spouse does not survive you, then Y will occur.

To understand this fully, you need to figure out what "survive" means. Somewhere in the will it will be defined, for example, to mean that a proposed beneficiary must survive you for 30 days.

Ask yourself whether enough contingencies are addressed in this way. So, if your spouse does not survive you (you die together in a joint accident), your will should provide for trusts for your children, but if they also don't survive you (they are in the same accident), you will want to provide for another level of beneficiaries.

It is up to you how far you go with this process, but you should seriously consider including at least three levels of beneficiaries, especially if you have a young family that often travels together.

You may wish to make a chart of the distribution on paper, like a decision tree, with the survival of each layer of beneficiaries being the centre of the branches.

Once you have reviewed the draft will a few times, don't drop the ball. The only thing worse than reading draft wills is having them sit on your counter for three months. Call the lawyer and let him or her know of any small changes, and arrange the next meeting.

Be sure you are clear whether you think you will be ready to sign at that meeting, or whether you want to revisit substantive issues in your will. Your lawyer will then be able to have the documents ready or will be prepared to discuss your further concerns and questions.

5. ACCEPT THAT THERE IS A REQUIRED PROCESS FOR SIGNING WILLS.

The rules about signing wills are intended to separate your scribbled notes about what you might like to happen at your death from the clear, written document that is indeed your last will and testment. The law attempts to do this by carefully prescribing the proper signing procedure for formal wills.

Formal wills must be signed by the "owner" of the will—referred to as "testator"—in the presence of two witnesses. All three people must be together at the same time. The testator usually signs first and then each witness signs. Since a will is often longer than one page, it is a good practice for a lawyer to have each of the three people initial each page of the will. This eliminates any suggestion that a page was added or substituted later.

When the testator dies, the last will may be required to be put through a court process called "probate," by which the court orders that indeed this is the deceased's last will. An important part of that process is showing the judge that the will was properly signed. This is done by filing an Affidavit of Execution sworn by one of the will's two witnesses, confirming under oath that the required signing procedure was followed.

The complexity of the signing procedure explains why your lawyer may be reluctant to send your final wills to your home or office for you to sign. As well, if neighbours or workmates are called in to act as the witnesses, it may be inconvenient for them to find a Commissioner of Oaths before whom they can swear to the truth of the contents of the Affidavit of Execution mentioned above. (To avoid problems in locating the witnesses after the death of the testator, the Affidavit of Execution is best completed within a few weeks of the signing of the wills.)

If you have been travelling or busy with other matters, your spouse may have acted as your intermediary with the lawyer, giving the lawyer your will instructions on your behalf. If so, don't be surprised if the lawyer wants to meet with you—without your spouse—before the will is signed, to ensure you understand the will and that it really reflects your wishes. Your lawyer does not distrust either you or your spouse—he or she is simply taking steps to prevent the possibility of coercion.

In a similar vein, there may be someone (maybe one of your children or a good friend) who has been actively involved in your will planning. For example, he or she may have recommended a lawyer, arranged the meetings, and taken you to the lawyer's office. The lawyer will likely not include that person in the meetings and, again, this is not a slight to that helpful person. The lawyer wants to ensure that, in the future, no one can suggest that the particular child or friend exercised undue influence in your estate planning process.

6. STORE YOUR ESTATE PLANNING DOCUMENTS IN A SAFE PLACE—AND LET THE EXECUTOR KNOW WHERE THAT IS!

A lot of great wills have never seen the light of day after they were signed—consider storing yours in the lawyer's wills vault or the trust company's vault (if you appointed a trust company as your professional executor). There is usually no charge for this service, and the firm or company may even contact you every few years to remind you about doing a review of your estate planning. Storing your will in your own safety deposit box or vault is fine if the executor knows where it is and how to get access to the safety deposit box or vault.

Avoid storing your precious original will in places such as under your bed or in your freezer. Loss by fire or theft can be rectified, of course, by doing a new will, but the fact that the will is missing may not be discovered until after your death or after you have lost competency and are, therefore, unable to sign a new will.

If only a copy of the will is found—after hunting high and low for the original—a court order can be sought, directing that the copy be treated like the original, but it is a complicated process, and your estate will be far better off if your executor can just find the original.

At the time you sign the will, you'll receive a copy of the signed original. This copy should have the location of the original will marked on it. Think twice about giving a copy to anyone, even your executor or beneficiaries. The executor should definitely have consented to being appointed and should know the location of the original will, but divulging the contents to the executor only means that you will have to keep him or her in the loop on any changes you make, unless you intend to surprise your executor when the "real last will" is pulled out.

Changes to wills can be sensitive—who knows, you might be changing the executor! So the safest route is to protect the privacy of your estate plan.

As always, there may be exceptions to this. For example, if your estate is very complex or you expect significant conflict, you and your advisers may decide that some level of disclosure before your death is wise.

Reviewing your will regularly is very important. Marriage, separation from your spouse, divorce, a move to another province or out of Canada, and the arrival of a child are all times when a will review is in order.

Writing your desired changes on a copy of the will, or the original will itself, is not a good idea at all—the changes may not even be legally effective!

Your will can be validly changed by either a codicil or a brand new will.

A codicil is usually quite short, stating that this is a codicil to the will that was signed on such-and-such a date, and then clearly setting out the change, such as deleting the paragraph appointing the executor and substituting a new paragraph with a new executor.

Changes more extensive than the executor or guardian appointment are best dealt with in a new will, both for clarity and privacy. If you are removing a beneficiary, for example, you likely don't want the old will, including the gift to the former beneficiary, to be disclosed at the time of your death. Making a new will ensures that the old will and all of its provisions are gone.

So there you have it—a plan to get that will signed (okay, at least started!). But like the Elderberry Gate Dinner Club, don't forget to keep it all in perspective ... *plan for the future, but remember to live in the moment!*

THE *Menu*

⌘

Quesadillas of smoked turkey, pickled red onions,
and Gouda cheese

Beef, black bean, and chayote squash chili

Savoury scones

Fresh pickled vegetables

Homemade vanilla ice cream

Pistachio-almond butter cookies

Chocolate pepper pretzels

⌘

Quesadillas of smoked turkey, pickled red onions, SERVES 8
   and Gouda cheese

¾ cup	grated medium or aged Gouda cheese, lightly packed	175 mL
⅓ cup	coarsely chopped smoked turkey	75 mL
¼ cup	chopped pickled red onion	50 mL
8	8-inch (20 cm) flour tortillas	8
8 tsp.	coriander chutney (see page 70)	40 mL

1. Toss together the Gouda, smoked turkey, and pickled red onions.

2. Lay out all 8 of the tortillas and spread 1 teaspoon (5 mL) of coriander chutney on each. Spread the filling evenly on one-half of each tortilla. Fold and press to flatten the quesadillas.

3. Cook in one of three ways:

    a. Preheat grill racks over a medium flame. Grill the quesadillas for a few minutes on each side, until the outside is crisp and the cheese is melted (watch carefully, as they are more prone to burning with this method).

    b. Heat a flat skillet or griddle pan over medium-high heat. Place the quesadillas on the ungreased surface, and cook until golden brown and crisp.

    c. Put the quesadillas on a baking sheet under a preheated broiler until they are golden brown and crisp, flipping them at least once during cooking (watch carefully, as they will brown quickly).

Pickled red onions

These crisp, intensely coloured onions are so delicious and versatile that you will never want to be without a jar on hand. Serve them in salads, sandwiches, chopped into meatloaf, in omelets, or in a roasted vegetable mélange. They elevate a burger like no commercial relish does.

1 cup	white vinegar	250 mL
1 tbsp.	salt	15 mL
2 cloves	garlic, cut in half, lengthwise	2 cloves
⅛ tsp.	dried oregano leaves	0.5 mL
½ tsp.	cracked black peppercorns	2 mL
¼ tsp.	sugar	1 mL
1	red onion, thinly sliced	1

1. Put the vinegar, salt, garlic, oregano, peppercorns, and sugar in a large jar or bowl. Stir to dissolve the salt and sugar.

2. Separate the onion slices and put them in a colander. Bring a kettleful of cold water to a boil and pour the boiling water over the onions.

3. Shake the colander gently to drain the onion slices and immediately transfer them to the vinegar mixture. Cover and refrigerate until cold and crisp with bright raspberry coloured edges, for at least 1 hour. The onions will keep for 2 weeks, refrigerated, though expect the colour to bleed.

Beef, black bean, and chayote squash chili   SERVES 8

Use meat from the shoulder (chuck or blade) of the beef. It is well marbled and retains its flavour and moisture throughout the lengthy cooking time, which would dry out a leaner cut.

	Bacon fat, for frying	
	All-purpose flour	
4 lb.	beef shoulder,	2 kg
	cut into 1-inch (2.5 cm) cubes	
1	large onion, diced	1
2 cloves	garlic, minced	2 cloves
1½ tbsp.	cumin	20 mL
2 tbsp.	Dutch process cocoa	25 mL
2 cups	peeled, seeded, finely chopped	500 mL
	tomatoes (fresh or canned)	
3 cups	beef stock	750 mL
1 bottle	dark beer	1 bottle
1 tsp.	dried oregano leaves *	5 mL
2	fresh jalapeño chilies, minced	2
2	chipotle** chilies, steeped for 15 minutes	2
	in very hot water, then minced	
	Salt and freshly ground black pepper	
4 cups	cooked black beans	1 L
4	chayote squash, peeled and diced	4

* Or 1 tbsp. (15 mL) fresh oregano leaves, toasted in a hot pan

** A smoked, dried jalapeño

1. Heat oven to 350°F (180°C).

2. Heat 1 tablespoon (15 mL) of bacon fat in a large, ovenproof skillet, over maximum heat. Coat a quarter of the beef cubes in flour and brown them in the hot oil. Transfer them to a large bowl. Repeat with the remaining beef, working with a quarter of the cubes each time. Do not wash the skillet.

3. In the same skillet, add more bacon fat. Cook the onions over medium heat, until transparent, then add the garlic, cumin, and cocoa. Transfer the beef and its juices back to the pan.

4. Add the tomatoes, beef stock, beer, oregano, jalapeños, and chipotle. Stir to blend, scraping the bottom of the pan to deglaze, and season with salt and pepper.

5. Cover and cook in the oven until the meat is tender, about 1½ to 2 hours, stirring every 30 minutes.

6. Add the black beans and chayote squash. Cook until the chayote is tender-crisp, about 30 minutes. Remove from the oven, check for flavour, cool to room temperature, and refrigerate overnight or up to 2 days. Reheat in a 350°F (180°C) oven for about 1 hour, until very hot.

Savoury scones   MAKES I DOZEN SCONES OR 3 DOZEN MINI SCONES

½	large onion, finely chopped	½
½ cup	cold butter, cut into ½-inch (1 cm) dice, plus 1 tbsp.	125 mL plus 15 mL
3 cups	all-purpose flour	750 mL
1 tbsp.	baking powder	15 mL
1 tbsp.	sugar	15 mL
½ tsp.	salt	2 mL
¼ tsp.	white pepper	1 mL
¾ cup	grated Gruyère cheese	175 mL
1 cup	buttermilk	250 mL
2	eggs, lightly beaten	2

1. Fry the onion in 1 tablespoon (15 mL) of butter until golden brown and tender.

2. Heat oven to 400°F (200ºC). In a large bowl whisk together the dry ingredients.

3. Cut in the ½ cup (125 mL) butter until the mixture resembles coarse meal, with some pea-sized pieces, then stir in the Gruyère.

4. In a separate bowl, combine the buttermilk, eggs, and onion. Pour the liquid mixture into the dry ingredients and stir gently with a fork until just blended. Do not over-mix.

5. Using an ice cream scoop, scoop out 12 even portions of the dough onto two ungreased baking sheets. Bake until the bottoms are golden brown, approximately 15 minutes.

Fresh pickled vegetables

1½ cups	rice vinegar or white wine vinegar	375 mL
1 tsp.	sambal oelek (see January, page 108)	5 mL
1 tbsp.	salt	15 mL
½ tsp.	coarsely ground black pepper	2 mL
1 tsp.	fresh basil	5 mL
12 to 15	French beans, tops and strings removed	12 to 15
1	small zucchini, cut in half lengthwise then in long, diagonal slices	1
1	small, yellow zucchini or crook neck squash, cut as zucchini	1
½	long English cucumber, cut into 3-inch (8 cm) long narrow strips	½
2	carrots, peeled and sliced into long diagonals	2
1	red or yellow sweet bell pepper, sliced lengthwise, ¼-inch (5 mm) thick	1
¼	red onion, sliced ⅛-inch (3 mm) thick	¼
2 cloves	garlic, sliced in half, lengthwise	2 cloves

1. Drop the beans into boiling, salted water and cook until slightly soft-ened, but still crisp, about 2 minutes.

2. In a large bowl, combine the rice vinegar, sambal oelek, salt, pepper, and basil. Stir until salt is dissolved. Add all of the vegetables and mar-inate at least 2 hours, and as long 24 hours.

Homemade vanilla ice cream   MAKES 1 QUART (1 L)

This recipe is for a basic vanilla ice cream and is easily adapted to suit most tastes and occasions. Add a double shot of espresso, chopped pistachios, fresh raspberries, ribbons of dark and white chocolate ganache, or bits of your favourite chocolate bar.

8	egg yolks	8
⅔ cup	sugar	150 mL
2 cups	milk	500 mL
2 cups	heavy cream (35% M.F.)	500 mL
2 tsp.	vanilla extract*	10 mL

* Purists should substitute three vanilla beans for the vanilla extract. Infuse the vanilla with the cream in step 2, allow to sit, covered and off the heat for 30 minutes. Scrape the pods into the cream mixture, reheat, and proceed.

1. In a large, heatproof bowl, whisk together the egg yolks and sugar.

2. In a heavy saucepan, heat the milk and cream on a medium-high burner until very hot, but not boiling.

3. Pour one-third of the milk-cream mixture into the egg yolks, whisking gently.

4. Return the milk-cream mixture to the burner, reduce heat to medium, and pour in the tempered yolks. Stir with a whisk until the mixture is thick enough to coat the back of a spoon. Strain and chill.

5. Proceed according to the instructions for your ice cream maker.

Cookies

Aside from tasting great, the primary advantage of both these cookies is that they do well to sit for a day before serving, making them part of a great do-ahead dessert.

Pistachio almond butter cookies

1 cup	butter	250 mL
¾ cup	sugar	175 mL
½ cup	long-thread coconut, sweetened or unsweetened	125 mL
½ tsp.	vanilla	2 mL
1½ cups	all-purpose flour	375 mL
½ tsp.	baking soda	2 mL
¼ tsp.	salt	1 mL
⅓ cup	sliced, unblanched almonds	75 mL
⅓ cup	chopped pistachios	75 mL

1. Heat oven to 350°F (180ºC).

2. Cream the butter and sugar. Add the coconut and vanilla. Mix well.

3. In a separate bowl, whisk together the flour, baking soda, and salt. Stir into the butter mixture, along with the almonds and pistachios.

4. Form into 1-inch (2.5 cm) balls, place 3 inches (8 cm.) apart on ungreased baking sheets, and press each ball to flatten slightly with the bottom of a cup, dipped in sugar.

5. Bake for 8 to 10 minutes, until just golden.

Chocolate pepper pretzels   MAKES 2 DOZEN COOKIES

¼ cup	Dutch processed cocoa powder	50 mL
½ tsp.	salt	2 mL
¼ tsp.	allspice	1 mL
½ tsp.	ginger	2 mL
½ tsp.	black pepper	2 mL
½ tsp.	white pepper	2 mL
½ cup	butter	125 mL
¾ cup	sugar	175 mL
1	egg	1
1 tbsp.	vanilla	15 mL
	Grated zest of 1 orange	
2 cups	flour	500 mL

1. Heat oven to 350°F (180ºC). Sift together the cocoa powder, salt, and spices. Set aside.

2. Cream together the butter and sugar.

3. Add the egg and mix well, scraping down the sides of the bowl. Add the chocolate mixture, vanilla, and orange zest. Beat until well mixed. Scrape the sides and bottom of the bowl.

4. Gradually add the flour and beat until smooth. Shape the dough into two cylinders, wrap in plastic, and refrigerate at least 1 hour.

5. Cut one cylinder into 12 equal pieces. Work each piece into a 10-inch (25 cm) long rope, as a child would make a snake out of play dough. Shape each "snake" into a pretzel shape and place it on an ungreased baking sheet. Repeat with the second cylinder of dough. Bake 20 to 25 minutes, until the pretzels are thoroughly cooked.

To decorate:

2 ounces	white chocolate	50 g
	Crystal sugar	

Melt the white chocolate and put it into a small plastic freezer bag. Snip off a corner of the bag and drizzle the white chocolate onto the pretzels in thin, diagonal stripes. Sprinkle generously with crystal sugar. Do not store the cookies until the white chocolate has set.

Advance Preparation

Aside from the scones, this entire menu was designed to be prepared a day or two in advance, then transported to the Enrights' cabin to be finished and served. For advance preparation of the scones, prepare the dry ingredients through step 3 and the wet ingredients through step 4. Store refrigerated, in separate containers until needed, then combine and finish.

RECIPE INDEX

SUBJECT INDEX